Relationships Matter

MANAGE YOUR THOUGHTS, FEELINGS AND ACTIONS TO DEVELOP AND MAINTAIN HEALTHY RELATIONSHIPS

NIMI KAY

COPYRIGHT

DEDICATION

To these very special relationships in my life:
My beautiful mother, whose inner strength has inspired me all
through my life

My wonderful loving husband for opening my heart to love,
for sharing life's most enriching experiences with me, and for
his unique talent to instantly connect with total strangers

The most cherished gift from God, my adorable, loving
children, and their loving spouses

My supportive siblings and their families, who have stood by
me through all challenges

My extended family of some of the most affectionate relatives
and friends who shower their unconditional love on me

A very special dedication to the two smiling little Angels, Shay
and Max,
who brighten me up with their purity and glow

I want to extend my heartfelt gratitude to all those beautiful
human beings who became part of my life's experience at
different stages of my life. I am grateful to them for enriching
my life by giving it the energy of their thoughts, feelings, and
actions.

I also want to thank all the motivators, gurus, and authors,
some of them mentioned in the book, who helped me on the
path to self-awakening.

TABLE OF CONTENTS

Introduction

Relationships make life worth living, and healthy relationships are a blessing. They enrich our lives and help us share a universal feeling of love. They validate our existence, our self-esteem; they nurture us and provide support when needed.

Motivation to succeed in life comes from our relationships—relationship with ourselves, relationship with a life partner, relationships with family members, friends, co-workers, teachers/mentors, with students, and fans or followers.

"The good life is built with good relationships," concluded Robert Waldinger at the end of one of the most-watched TED Talks.

Waldinger's talk was on "What makes a good life? Lessons from the longest study on happiness." In his presentation, Robert Waldinger, director of an ongoing Harvard Study of adult development, shared these highlights:

- Though most of us aspire to be rich and famous, it is not money or fame that gives us humans a sense of a fulfilling life and ultimate happiness. It is the quality of our relationships with other humans that determines how fulfilling our life is.
- People with healthy and happy relationships live

longer irrespective of their financial and social status.
- One in five Americans suffers from the feeling of loneliness due to a lack of healthy, caring, nurturing relationships in their lives.

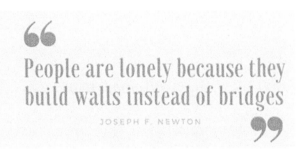

People are lonely because they build walls instead of bridges

JOSEPH F. NEWTON

Unfortunately, some of us, at times, feel dejected, let down, or bound and helpless in relationships and in circumstances.

I have met many people who have said things like:

"I am so nice to my friends / family members. I help them in whatever way I can. I call them so very often. I treat them to nice meals, write them cards, buy them gifts, but still I don't know why they are not pleased with me. Why I cannot have lasting relationships. Is something wrong with me?"

"I am such a hard worker. I stay late at work, yet my employer is not happy with me. It causes me so much stress."

"I am not happy in my marriage because my husband is not what I expected him to be. He does not understand me, does not know what I want from life . . . I think he is cheating on me....he does not listen to me, does not care for me. I don't know what to do to be happily married."

> 66
> **Relationships are more important than life, but it is important for those relationships to have life in them...**
>
> SWAMI VIVEKANANDA
> 99

Most of us face relationship challenges at some time in our lives and then end up feeling dejected. These feelings often result from thoughts like: "I love someone, but they don't love me back," or "I work hard at my job, but I'm not appreciated." We are hurt, and we feel rejected or angry. We may get into a defensive or revenge mode. All these feelings drain our energy. We want to stay away from these energy-drainers as they don't take us forward. We so yearn for emotions that energize us and make us feel loved.

So, what do we do in such situations when we feel hurt, dejected, and unappreciated or unloved?

Well, I have personally experienced these feelings at different stages of my life, and at times, they made me miserable, angry, frustrated, mistrusting, and suspicious of others' intentions. And as a result of my feelings, I lost opportunities to have meaningful and strong friendships and bonds. I also lost time and energy that I could have spent in a joyful state, or on experiences that would have made life more fulfilling.

It got to a point where I felt I *needed* to stop the energy drainage of negative thoughts and feelings—if not for the sake of my relationships, at least for my sanity. It affected my health. If I discussed my uneasiness with someone, I was advised to seek therapy, or consult a doctor, which made me feel worse and more confused about my feelings. I have nothing against seeking therapy or seeing a doctor. I am sure it is helpful. However, I personally did not feel comfortable to go that route for these two reasons. First, it meant labeling myself as a patient who is suffering from a disease. And second, in my opinion, changing a mindset is an ongoing long-term process that one can be successful at only by understanding *self* better, and by changing one's thinking.

Hence I set out to find my own solution.

I started researching to understand what was causing these feelings and how I could correct them. I read lots of books-*The Secret* by Rhonda Byrne, *The Game of Life and How to Play It* by Florence Scovel Shinn, *The Power of Now* by Eckhart Tolle, *The Seven Spiritual Laws of Success* by Deepak Chopra, and *How to Win Friends and Influence People* by Dale Carnegie. I also listened to many motivational speakers who teach the art of living and managing relationships.

My biggest takeaway from all this reading and listening was:

All this suffering was happening because of my thoughts and the frequency of my energy. My thoughts were creating the feelings I was experiencing, and my perceptions were creating a particular image of my relationships. The realization that it was entirely in my hands to stop such feelings from cropping up and making me miserable was empowering.

If you look closely at all the examples of unhappy relationships, you notice one constant pattern in all the scenarios. The person complaining of an unhappy relationship is seeking joy and happiness from others' actions and reactions. "He doesn't love me anymore" translated means "I will be happy only if he loves me." "Others don't appreciate my work" means "I will be happy only if others appreciate my work." "No one understands me" means "I will be happy only if others understand me."

They expect others to do something to provide them the happiness they are looking for. They presume that their real experience will match their perception of a happy relationship only when others behave a certain way. But in reality, their expectations will be like a mirage—now I see it, now I don't—and will cause friction and misunderstandings in their relationships.

The expectation that others' behavior will bring happiness is so inhibiting. It means their happiness is always dependent on others' actions. They have given others the power to control their state of mind.

It is at times like this, when one feels a lack of love and appreciation from expected sources, that one seeks solace in other external pleasures, such as smoking, drinking, drugs, and sex. And the harder one tries to find happiness in these pleasures, the shallower a person feels inside. These habits are more like escape routes, and they indicate that a person does not want to face real-life issues, such as lack of self-esteem or self-love. The person is so detached from their inner self that they feel hollow inside. This is when the feeling of doubt "maybe they love me, maybe not," starts showing up and confusing the person.

Once this realization dawned that my expectations of life and my reality had a big gap and that I had handed over the control of my state of mind to others, it was quite an awakening. On introspection, I discovered that it was true—I was always seeking love or approval from others. I was trying to please others to get to that mirage of "their love and appreciation." It never occurred to me that it was in my hands to feel good about myself, to create a feeling of self-appreciation.

I also learned that I needed to be more aware of my thoughts to manage my life better. I needed to acquire skills to manage my thoughts, feelings, and actions; and I needed to manage my expectations in relationships better. Gradually, I started implementing some of the lessons learned.

Making this awareness part of my day-to-day life needed ongoing effort and continuous practice. I also had to put in a conscious effort to understand my relationships, or rather, how I thought about my relationships and what I expected from them.

I started on this journey of self-awareness with a single-minded focus, and after some time, it brought about a significant shift in my perspective. I became a new person. I smiled and laughed more often; I felt more confident and comfortable interacting with others. What it did for me was really very impressive. My relationships with my husband, family members, friends, and co-workers improved a lot. I no longer feared being judged; I no longer felt dejected or not good enough; I no longer got irritated or frustrated with anyone. I became quite fearless. And the most pleasant change that I felt was that others enjoyed my company and wanted to share experiences with me.

However, I did become selective about my friendships, new partnerships, and interactions; and it was by choice. Once I chose to pursue certain relationships, I made an unconditional commitment to them and nurtured them. The approach I adopted was to focus on my feelings of love toward others and not look for love and appreciation in return. I got rid of my dependency on others' love and validation to feel happy. It became my choice to share my love for others instead of waiting on others to love and appreciate me. I stopped looking for validation from others for my words and actions. I learned to value myself; I learned to recognize my skills and talents and respect myself for being me. And this felt like a new kind of freedom I had not known earlier.

Now, you may be wondering how I brought about this major change. I have been working on this self-enhancement effort for over a decade, and it is still a work in progress.

Expecting a change overnight or in a few days is not realistic. It requires a shift in personality, which means changing habits of thinking, feeling, and doing things in a certain way, habits that have been acquired over a long period. To make this change, you need to be determined, focused, and disciplined to replace old habits with new ones. You need to allocate some time and energy to bring about this change.

If you want to know what specific steps I took on this journey of shifting my perspective and becoming a more joyful person, please read further to know more about the process of managing your thoughts, feelings, and actions to develop and maintain long-lasting and meaningful relationships. Part 1 of this book talks about general rules applied in day-to-day life to build and maintain healthy relationships. Part 2 focuses on the specific nuances and challenges in a marriage. Part 3 elaborates on scenarios in friendships and at work and how best to manage relationships with friends and co-workers.

The first few chapters provide tips on how to steer your

thoughts in the right direction so that they generate constructive energy. The next few chapters talk about recognizing this energy in motion means acknowledging your emotions. And finally, how to use this productive energy in your actions to move forward on your desired path to healthy relationships.

Part 1

General Rules to Build, Develop and Maintain Healthy Relationships

Here are some of the steps that I took very consciously in my approach to developing and maintaining healthy relationships with everyone. These rules can be applied as general rules for all types of relationships.

CHAPTER ONE

Improve Relationship with Yourself

First and foremost, you need to have a healthy relationship with yourself and your immediate surroundings.

You cannot have a healthy relationship with others if you do not have a healthy relationship with yourself. You cannot expect others to love and respect you if you yourself, in your subconscious mind, have doubts about your worthiness, do not trust your own intuition and judgment, or are indecisive most of the time.

> **"**
>
> ## The most important decision you will ever make is to be in a good mood.
>
> VOLTAIRE
>
> **"**

How do you have a healthy relationship with yourself?

Improve your relationship with yourself by knowing yourself better, by having clarity about your life's purpose, by accepting yourself completely for who you are, by accepting your circumstances without resistance, and by loving and respecting yourself.

You want to get up every day feeling good about yourself, eager to experience another wonderful day that life has to offer you.

How do you learn to appreciate yourself?

Initially, you have to make a conscious effort to develop this feeling of self-love. Then, it becomes a part of your personality.

Conscious steps in this direction would be to first look closely at your personality type, thoughts, and feelings, and then to create and implement a plan of action to make desired changes in your habits and perceptions.

1. Get to know yourself better

Be aware of your thoughts and your personality type.

An average human creates a minimum of eighteen thousand thoughts in a given day. And some overthinking personalities may be creating about sixty thousand thoughts in a day.

Some philosophers have categorized thoughts into four types:

Positive thoughts – these are thoughts that generate good feelings, are pure in nature, and don't have any strong emotions attached to them. These thoughts energize us and motivate constructive actions.

Negative thoughts – these are thoughts that come from ego and from a feeling of fear and insecurity. They have strong emotions attached to them, such as worry, jealousy, hate, anger, disgust, guilt, or fear. These thoughts can be most taxing on your energy and your health. They can stress your body, move it into fight-or-flight mode, or make you experience overdrive and burnout. For example, worrying about another's opinion of you is a negative thought. It makes you uneasy and uncomfortable. It does not motivate you to take a constructive action. Rather it lowers your morale and affects the task at hand adversely.

Action thoughts – these are considered necessary thoughts and are most productive in nature. You create these thoughts to perform an action, to create something, or when you are fully engaged in the task at hand.

Waste thoughts – these are thoughts about your past or your future, and they are totally futile. You cannot change your past. By thinking of the past incidents, you are making it your present because you are recreating the same emotions.

It is OK to learn some lessons from your past mistakes, or to think of pleasant memories of the past to generate similar good feelings in the present. Other than that, thoughts of the past, particularly of the unpleasant experiences, are of no use. And there is no certainty of the future that you create with your imaginative thoughts if you do not take right action in the present.

To summarize, our positive thoughts and our action thoughts are the most useful and productive. We should focus on these two types of thoughts. Or rather, our effort should be to create these thoughts consciously.

Successful people either naturally tend to focus on positive thoughts, or they train themselves to engage their energies on creating these two types of thoughts.

There is a belief that our thoughts become things. To elaborate, our thoughts generate certain feelings. These feelings motivate us to say certain things or perform specific actions; repeated actions of a particular type become habits, and habits make our personalities. Personalities can be varied: joyful or sulking, introverted or extroverted, confident or shy, and so on. Right from birth, many factors contribute to personality formation. I will not delve into discussing all those influences here. However, I will emphasize that quite a few of our habits that develop over time and form our personality can be changed with a conscious, committed effort.

Growing up, I mostly looked sad and melancholy. Even though I don't remember feeling sad, relatives and teachers would sometimes ask me why I looked sad. I don't know what the cause of my melancholic disposition was. Was it because I lost my father when I was just five, or was it that I didn't look as pretty as the most popular girl in my class? My effort to do well in my studies and be top in the class probably was a sign that I was seeking validation through my good performance in school to make up for the love and appreciation that I felt was missing in my life.

Once I became an adult and started working, I didn't like it if anyone asked, "Why do you look sad?" I did not want to have that disposition. I started working on changing my personality. And now, despite some extremely challenging life situations, it has been years since anyone asked, "Why do you look so sad?"

To know your personality type, you will need to observe yourself from a distance. You will need to be more conscious of your thoughts and feelings in changing situations throughout the day. You will need to be aware of your reactions to changing situations. How do you feel soon after waking up? What are you thinking while attending to daily chores? What is going through your mind when interacting with family members and taking care of children? How do you feel going to work, attending work meetings, or attending social gatherings? What thoughts come to your mind, and what kind of emotions do you feel? Are you anxious about not being on time, not doing your best? Are you conscious of being judged for your looks, for your work, or your skill level? Do you feel nervous or confident while interacting with others? Do you get angry often, or are you the tolerant type? Are you always judging others? Are you critical of others? Are you sensitive to what others say about you? Do you have some lingering fears of not being successful at your endeavors, of losing in a competition? Or are you always optimistic and expecting good results?

Try to tune into your thoughts. Your thoughts influence your body's reaction to certain situations. Your body will show signs of your feelings, or your actions and words will express the emotions generated as a result of your thoughts.

If you feel low on energy, don't feel motivated to complete tasks on hand, or are getting annoyed with others, then it is your thoughts that are making you feel like this. Similarly, if you feel excited and joyful about some upcoming event or are enjoying what you are doing in the present moment, then this feeling is also being generated by your thoughts.

During this process focus should be to observe the pattern of thoughts and not to identify the origin of these thoughts. Trying to identify the origin of thoughts, such as an incident of the past, can be helpful, but quite painful in case of thoughts that are attached with unhappy memories. At the same time if you notice that thoughts of those sad incidents are coming up too frequently and causing you pain and affecting your behavior, then you need to address it in your plan of action. You will need to accept it and release yourself from its bondage.

By paying close attention to the pattern of your thoughts you will know your personality.

Once you have identified your personality type, you will need to own it wholeheartedly without being judgmental. Be willing to accept that many factors contributed to making you who you are today. There is no point in trying to figure out the causes and put the blame on someone, credit someone else for it, or feel guilty about choosing the wrong path at some stage in your life.

You are really lucky and certainly a very happy individual if your analysis indicates that you have exactly the kind of personality you admire and respect. You do not need this book because I am sure you are very happy with your relationships in your life.

Tips provided in this book are for those who believe they may develop stronger relationships by making certain changes in their personality and by changing their perspective of things in their life.

Suppose you want to change your disposition from an insecure, timid person to a confident person or from a sad nature to a happy spirit. You will have to put in extra effort to change your personality. It requires awareness of your personality/disposition and then a plan of action.

2. Recognize your feelings

I had a boss who, when asked, "Dan, how are you this morning?" would always reply cheerfully, "Couldn't be better". This made a great impression on me. I would think to myself, "This one expression in itself is so powerful in conveying his personality type. He is in the present moment and is also very confident that what he is feeling is his best feeling."

You may question, "Well that could just be the way he

generally responded to that question. He may not be actually feeling the best." Well, just because I was so impressed by it, I wanted to incorporate it as my habit too. But it did not come easily to me. I would stop to question myself, "Am I really feeling my best?" and then I would hesitate to say, "Couldn't be better."

This hesitation was an indicator that I did not believe I could be feeling my best at any given moment. I always felt short of that "best" feeling, as if it was going to come sometime, somewhere in the future. That shows there was potential for me to uplift my feelings, to do something that would make me feel my best at a given moment. That is the difference between a happy, confident disposition and an unhappy, uncertain disposition. My guess is (I never got courage to ask Dan) that Dan probably worked on his mindset so he could say, "Couldn't be better" every morning. He genuinely felt good about himself all the time, irrespective of the circumstances. Here is an example to illustrate that.

For a month or so, after Dan had a minor accident that injured his one foot, he would come to office using crutches. Even during that period, when someone asked Dan, "How are you?" his answer would be, "Couldn't be better."

To get started on the path of feeling good about yourself, you need to follow certain steps, have a plan of action to make your personality to be the one that you love and that others also love and respect.

In this plan of action, you will need to incorporate a strategy to change your thinking habits and your reactions, and you must choose your words consciously to uplift your spirits and the spirits of those around you.

CHAPTER TWO

Plan of Action

Here are some tips that can help on this journey of improving your relationship with yourself.

1. Accept yourself unconditionally

After defining your personality type and knowing your feelings better, you will realize that you may have been harsh in describing yourself. We all tend to judge ourselves more harshly compared to judging others. So, if you want to improve your relationship with yourself, you need to accept every part of yourself as unique to you without attaching any negative or positive emotions to it, without attaching pride or shame to it.

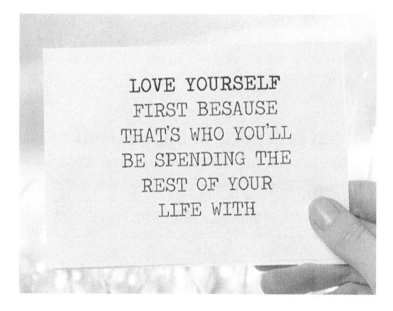

Accept your looks—tall, short, fat, slim, fair, dark—as being special to you. Accept all past incidents of your life, happy or unhappy, as experiences that created your life and made you who you are today, without any emotions attached to them. Accept all your personality traits—aggressive, slow, ambitious, impulsive, arrogant, meek, hardworking, or lazy. Recognize them, but also own them without any judgment. It will help in taking the next step of making habit changes to get your desired results. Then you will not attach any emotions to your efforts.

You will consciously make certain changes just because you think it will help you in improving your perception of yourself. It is OK to change habits to feel good about yourself, to achieve certain goals in relationships or in your career, as long as you do not attach emotions, such as "once I do this I will be loved more," to the end result.

Instead, just enjoy the process itself. The focus has to be on changing habits and not beating yourself up for having a personality you don't like. You do not have to feel ashamed or guilty for anything. Remember, you are doing this to change your perception of you and not to impress others.

2. Feel good about yourself

I am sure every now and then you come across a person who does not hesitate to say, "I am the best." You may or may not believe them, but you do admire their confidence in themselves. Their perception of their ability to do something is very close to what they expect from themselves.

This illustration titled "Happiness Is a State of Mind" in an Instagram post by "Billionaire Behaviour" depicts this very well. Whether you are first or third in a competition, it is up to you to put yourself in a happy state of mind, which mostly depends on what outcome you expected from the competition in the first place. Was it the fun of participating, or just getting to the number one position?

Assign time to do introspection. During this time, you will need to analyze exactly what is bothering you. Have clarity on your life's purpose, your goals, and your desires in all areas of your life: career, marriage, romance, or other partnerships. Where is the gap in your expectations of yourself and your current state in these areas? You will need to reduce this gap between your expectations and your perceptions of everything in your life.

Create a plan to make a *conscious effort on a daily basis of creating new thoughts that will help reduce this gap in your expectations and your reality. The plan should include the steps of uplifting your morale, your confidence.* This can be done in many ways (depending on what you are seeking), such as feeling good about your looks, your personality traits, your professional skills, or your presentation skills. This may include taking classes, adding to your knowledge, acquiring a new skill, or getting experience in a specific field.

Then you need to incorporate this plan of action in your daily life by assigning time to doing things that make you feel good about yourself and raise your self-esteem. You could start every morning by looking at yourself in the mirror and saying, "You are beautiful, and you are smart and unique. You are in this world to fulfill a specific purpose. You have the required skills or will acquire the required skills to fulfill that purpose. You are a loving and caring person. Others love you and respect you for who you are."

3. Admire yourself for your personality, your talents, skills, and good nature

Dr. Deepak Chopra recommends this approach of saying three affirmations every time you look in a mirror. He calls it mirror technique. I wrote them on a piece of paper and stuck it to my bathroom mirror so I can read them every morning.

- *I am independent of good or bad opinions of others.*
- *I am neither superior nor beneath anyone.*
- *I am fearless in the face of all challenges.*

Then have a mantra attached to this ritual. It could be any one word or a few words. Examples include "Aa Hum," which means "I am," and "Amen" meaning "let it be so."

Add this ritual as a task that you need to do a few times every day. And after a few days, you may answer like Dan when asked, "How are you feeling?"

Dr. Chopra explains that your expectations determine the outcomes of your actions. As long as you don't attach emotions to the outcome, your expected outcome is determined. If you are not getting expected results, it means you are attaching emotions to that result.

For example, if you desire to win a competition, and you are confident that you have practiced enough, that you have acquired all the skills, and that you are the most eligible candidate, you will most certainly win unless a fear of losing suddenly chokes you while still in the game. I remember listening to a podcast where a celebrity athlete describes how she did not get selected to participate in the Olympics despite being a top performer because she suddenly choked when she looked at the selection committee midway through her game, and got distracted with fearful thoughts.

The same principle applies to our behavior in our daily interactions. Our behavior is mostly guided by our inner dialogue. If our inner dialogue debates our eligibility as a winner, and in our mind we doubt we can win, then the win is not going to happen.

Dr. Chopra further explains that our body's cells are eavesdropping on our inner dialogue all the time. Whatever we express through our internal dialogue is conveyed to our body's cells, and our body takes action to manifest the outcome of the dialogue. For example, if you are worrying about something, your body starts showing signs of stress. As a result, instead of finding a solution to what you are worrying about, your body gets into action to deal with the stress and this becomes a big energy drainer. Similarly, if your thoughts are predominantly of some perceived impending danger and you are feeling fearful, your physical faculties are going to be less prepared to deal with the danger. Thoughts that create worry, fear or other similar negative feelings make us less productive and lower our energy levels.

The question then is, "How do we guide this inner dialogue so that it works in our favor to get positive outcomes?"

The most challenging part here is that it is not easy to train our mind to stop thinking unless we practice meditation. And even then, one can control thoughts only for a short duration, while in meditation, and not all through the day.

Well-known neuroscientist Andrew Huberman, in one of his interviews, provides this suggestion: "It is hard to suppress thoughts, but it is easier to introduce new thoughts." Hence, the best way to guide your thoughts in your desired direction is to intentionally create new thoughts that are in alignment with your desires. That is why, sometimes, it is helpful to articulate and write your desires, because it helps steer your thoughts in that direction. And then your body's cells start listening to these new thoughts.

Make your own personal list of some affirmations that can be used to replace thoughts of worry and fear. Here are some examples by Florence Scovel Shinn:

I am harmonious, poised and magnetic. I now draw to myself my own. My power is God's power and is irresistible.

The tide of destiny has turned and everything comes my way.

The "four winds of success" now blow to me my own. From North, South, East and West comes my endless good.

The decks are now cleared for Divine Action and my own comes to me under grace in a magical way.

Divine order is established in my mind body and affairs.

4. Take care of your body

I have seen some people taking better care of their cars than their bodies. Both serve you on your life's journey. However, your body is your primary vehicle to serve you on your life's journey. Your body's health and fitness is of utmost importance in the context of fulfilling your dreams and in generating desired feelings. I am not talking about how your body looks. I am talking about how your body feels.

A car that looks very attractive but has a weak or dead engine will not get you far. Similarly, looking beautiful externally is no guarantee to feeling good if your internal systems are not working well. Improving your external appearance does nothing more than boost your ego, which may somewhat help you in improving self-esteem. But having all your internal systems working efficiently as well as a healthy emotional state are more important. Your emotional resilience is also largely dependent on your physical health. Emotional and physical health are codependent. The health of one impacts the health of the other.

So you, in no way, are being selfish if you take care of your health by eating well, sleeping, and exercising enough to keep your body functioning. A healthy body is better equipped to generate good feelings. It is your responsibility as a human to take care of your body.

I have made a conscious effort to prioritize personal care and healthy eating in all circumstances. Incorporating certain habit changes is not about time or resources. It is more about intention and motivation. Once you start having a strong belief that you need your body in good health to serve you well in achieving your goals, you will find the intention and motivation to incorporate healthy habits.

Taking good care of their children is every parent's priority. You should treat your body as your first child. This thought will motivate you to nurture your body and not ignore your body's needs. I sometimes tell myself, "Hey, it is Nimi's lunch time. What are you feeding her? Hope it is healthy." or "Nimi needs good nourishment. Don't ignore her."

Here are some suggestions about a mindful approach for daily health-care rituals.

Most of us brush our teeth and wash our bodies on a daily basis. I will not be talking about such rituals here. I recommend including a few additional habits.

With the new day comes
new strength and new thoughts.

Eleanor Roosevelt

✓ Instead of waking with an alarm, learn to let your body's circadian rhythm guide you to wake up. A circadian rhythm or circadian cycle is a natural, internal process that regulates the sleep–wake cycle and repeats roughly every twenty-four hours. This is the best way to show respect for your body first thing in the morning. Waking with an alarm causes a bit of anxiety at the very start of the day. First, if you already snoozed it a few times after the initial alarm, you have very subtly added a feeling of guilt for not following through with your plan. Second, if you are waking with a jerk, especially if your body is not well rested, it is not a good signal to your body to perform optimally through the day. I am not suggesting that you miss your important morning meetings trying to follow the circadian rhythm. If you have been waking with an alarm all your life, then it is going to take some effort to change that pattern. Try to implement it gradually, may be by starting on days when you don't have morning meetings or on weekends.

✓ For the first five minutes after waking up, pay attention to your breathing. Consider it a short meditation to guide your thoughts for the day.

✓ Spend a few minutes appreciating and taking care of your sensory organs (eyes, ears, skin, nose, etc.) that help you all through the day in creating new perceptions about the world.

✓ Adding a short daily workout to stretch your limbs and move your joints will make your body more agile and well-regulated. This is a way to show respect to your body's systems.

✓ Do not miss your morning or evening walk or exercise. If you are pressed for time, it is OK to do it for a few minutes rather than not doing at all.

✓ *Eat food as medicine, otherwise you will be consuming medicine as food* - Instead of depending on doctors to treat you if something goes wrong with your body, educate yourself about essential nutrients (vitamins and minerals) your body needs. Learn what foods provide these nutrients. Be mindful of what you eat and drink and what effect they have on your body. Do not depend on a family member to determine what is right for your body. Be a conscious decision maker in choosing food for your body. Do not eat for the sake of filling your stomach or to satisfy your taste buds. Eat to provide your body with fuel so that it can generate energy to perform actions you want it to perform, to serve your life's purpose.

The above-mentioned suggestions will be effective only when followed consciously and performed as a ritual without fail.

5. Love, respect, and trust yourself

If you are confident that you put in your best effort yesterday, and you will put in your best effort today, with full integrity, in whatever you do at work, at home, and while interacting with others then you will wake up feeling good each morning. Using your energies optimally to take care of things that matter to you, and to get positive results in your endeavors and interactions, will contribute to your well-being.

And all this is possible when you are aware of your desires, energy levels, thoughts, words, and actions all through the day. You just need to stay attuned to your own thoughts with clear intention and purposeful approach. Let your thoughts be more focused on the task you are performing than on unhappy incidents of the past or on some imaginary fears about your future.

Once in tune with these thoughts, you will enjoy doing all your daily tasks, however mundane or boring they may be, and you will have a great sense of achievement by the end of the day. You can't help but fall in love with yourself. You will feel a boost in self-esteem, which will protect you from settling for less in relationships.

Self-respect is important. Others respect you only when you respect yourself. "Respect is earned, not demanded." If you believe in this saying, then you need to first earn your own respect, before expecting respect from others. So, to respect yourself, you need to find qualities in yourself that would earn your respect, be it your knowledge, your skills, your disposition, your self-discipline, your sense of humor, your hardworking personality, or your life experiences. You need to respect who you are as a person and respect what you do.

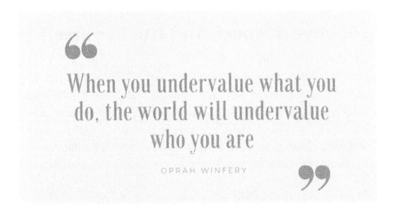

When you undervalue what you do, the world will undervalue who you are

OPRAH WINFERY

If you are not able to find qualities worth loving and respecting in yourself, then you need to do further introspection and add qualities that would earn your love and respect. To be successful in this effort, you need to have full faith in yourself and believe that you can become whatever you desire to be as a person. In this approach, do not include your looks, which came to you genetically, or changed due to situations out of your control; and don't waste your energies on thinking negatively about that aspect of yourself. You are way bigger and more important than mere physical beauty.

> **You don't become what you want. You become what you believe you can become**
>
> OPRAH WINFERY

Have faith that you are a person who others gravitate to. Visualize yourself as having the best relationships. Family members love you, and you get to experience good things in others' company. Others elevate your energies and respect you. You get the most joy from doing things for others.

6. Be fully engaged with your immediate surroundings

We spend most of our time at two places: home and school/workplace, depending on what stage of life we are at. Each one of us calls some place home—a place where we feel at ease and safe, where we eat, relax, and entertain ourselves, where we spend time with family and create many memories that stay with us forever. It is our responsibility to respect and care for this space.

We want to create a space that uplifts our mood, inspires us, and motivates us. And that is possible when we are fully engaged with it, when we treat it as an integral part of our well-being. It goes without saying that the majority of us do treat our homes well. The reason I am mentioning it here is because we, as a society, are dealing with a cluttered-life syndrome—with too much of middle-class abundance—and at times that is overwhelming many people. Too many unnecessary things that we don't even need add clutter to our life.

The energy and effort we spend on taking care of these materialistic things that we don't really need for building a happy life could be better spent enjoying and sharing experiences with others and on creating a feeling of love that is so essential for our life.

7. You are what you consume, so consume carefully

Your body's health largely depends on what you eat. However, your overall emotional and physical health depends on everything that you consume —food as well as information that you receive through various media platforms all through the day (books, TV, emails, speeches, and social media) influence your emotional state, that further effects your physical health. This information overload through various media platforms and electronic devices is taking away our time at home or at work that could be spent on productive activities and general growth.

You need to be aware of what kind of information you are consuming and what type of feelings it is generating within you. What emotions are you experiencing: love or hate, rage or peace, sadness or happiness, hope or frustration? So often what you see happening as part of someone else's life (be it in the news, in a book, or a movie) influences you. It creates a memory attached with a specific emotion in your brain and your body cells. In most instances, your preconditioning is affected to such an extent that you believe similar circumstances will have similar results in your life too. Which is not always true. For example, if one is used to watching soap operas that show spouses cheating in their marriages, one is likely to get a thought that their spouse could also be cheating on them, or maybe they begin to believe it is OK to cheat in marriage. With a seed of suspicion and this kind of thought, this person has already started growing a subtle rift in their relationship. And, as a result, even if their spouse is the most loyal person, this individual will always treat the relationship with some degree of suspicion.

We, as a society, are so used to consuming content, just because it is free; or we don't mind seeing targeted ads in between our favorite programs because we are hooked to those programs. Seeing a commercial about a pharma product repeatedly is going to make you think, even though in a detached way, about the underlying disease it is meant for. Why does one need to waste one's thoughts on such irrelevant things?

So often, to justify their consumption of this kind of information, people will say, "Oh no, it doesn't affect me that way. I am watching it in a very detached way, just for entertainment." This response comes from a conscious mind. They don't realize that their subconscious mind does not know they are watching in a detached way. That information is still going to record in their subconscious with emotions attached to it.

These kinds of influences from external information sources are very subtle, but can be powerful enough to form personalities and to make or break relationships.

8. Incorporate an attitude of gratitude

Be grateful for the relationships that already exist in your life. Consider yourself lucky and blessed if you have close relations (family and friends) who give you unconditional love and care for you. Don't ever take them for granted. Be sensitive to their feelings and their needs. Nurture these relationships with tolerance and understanding. Accept that everyone is unique and has a specific purpose in life. They are also part of your purpose of life. Honor these relationships with unconditional love, without any expectations or judgments.

> **Be thankful for what you have; you will end up having more. If you concentrate on what you don't have, you will never have enough**
>
> OPRAH WINFERY

They may irritate you or get upset with you at times. But they do enrich your life. Life is interesting and worth living because of these relationships.

CHAPTER THREE

Choose the Relationships You Want to Pursue

This chapter, instead of focusing on thoughts and feelings, talks of actions you can take to choose right relationships in your life. Though these actions are also a result of your thoughts. These thoughts are considered necessary thoughts to move forward, to manifest your desires.

Be clear about who you want to interact with and have a long-term relationship with. Do some introspection before making a long-term commitment.

Here, I am not talking of relations with immediate family—parents, children, and siblings—with whom you have a blood relationship and live with for long periods of your life. Family relationships are not by choice; they are given to us by nature. These blood relationships are often strongest, and the reason for that is not the blood, but our tendency for unconditional love toward them, which comes naturally in these relationships. Personality differences, disagreements, and different approaches (because of external influences) are part of these relationships. But still that unconditional love, which may not be so apparent at times, is the bonding agent. One can use the same tendency of unconditional love in other relationships, too, with friends, spouses, in-laws, and colleagues.

Outside of immediate family, other than accidental short encounters at public places, social gatherings, and family get-togethers, you have a choice as to whom you want to develop a relationship with, personal or professional. Choose them carefully.

When you meet someone new, instead of analyzing their qualities, creating a profile in your mind about their appearance or body language, and judging their personalities, try to assess how you feel in their presence. Once you tune into this feeling it will provide answers to some relevant questions: Does their presence make you feel good? Does it give you an energizing feeling, a feeling of love? Or does it evoke negative feelings, such as fears of being judged, being looked down upon, or being rejected? Do they make you feel inadequate, awkward, or incompetent? Are they interacting with you out of sympathy or some selfish intention, or are they someone who is generally nice to everyone and genuinely cares for people?

Most of the time you are attracted to people who give you a feeling of love. But many a time, influenced by your preconceptions and external influences of societal fabric, you do not get clear signs of your feelings from your mind and body. That is why you need to put in effort to tune into the vibration of your real feelings. Have you heard the expression "gut feeling"? It is a meaningful expression for a reason. Our gut feelings tell us our real vibration. How we feel in our gut during an experience is quite a good indicator of our real inner feelings in a given situation.

Once you have clarity on your real feelings during an interaction, it will be easier for you to pick the relationships you want to pursue. Do not hesitate to pursue the relationships that you think will enrich your life. Go all out to make the first move, introduce yourself and start the conversation. At the same time, if you feel uneasy in any way, it is advisable to take time to know the person better.

There are also souls that have strong faith in the Universal energies to work in their favor and they believe that Universe will place them in the company of people most compatible to them. I think sometimes being in the flow with the Universal energies does help and can be quite rewarding if the belief is very strong. But challenge is to hold that strong belief, and then accept the results with total submission.

However hard you may wish that everyone was nice, and that you could get along with everyone, it just does not happen like that in the real world. You face many surprises when relationships do not turn out as you would have liked. There is no guarantee that every relationship you get into will be great. But that shouldn't deter you from forming relationships. You will definitely be doing yourself a favor by spending time and energy on choosing the right connections and being selective about who you want to have a relationship with.

We all know that there are consequences of getting into the wrong relationship, whether we have suffered those consequences personally or have seen someone close to us experience them. The severity of these consequences may vary from case to case. You may also wonder why one had to go through it. "I wish I had known the other person better before getting into the relationship."

The unfortunate part is that you get so carried away with the initial excitement of finding another human you can connect with that you don't pause to check anything else. You jump to making commitments without much thought. Sometimes, you do not take enough time to know the other person; other times you don't even want to worry about consequences because you are enjoying the company and want more of it. So you rush to make commitments.

We talked about recognizing your own personality type in Chapter 1. It will help you a great deal in getting into the right kinds of relationships if you can identify the personality type of the person you are about to build a relationship with. This is discussed in the context of marriage in Part 2, but I would like to mention a few personality types here. These are the personality types that you should recognize, if possible, before making any kind of commitment, be it in career decisions or long-term friendships.

You may say, "This does not go with the advice of following your gut feeling." Due to complexities of different personality types, sometimes our gut feelings can fail us. That is the reason I want to suggest getting to know another person better before making a commitment, especially if they show any signs of the personality types mentioned in this section.

Just being aware of your thoughts and feelings may not suffice to recognize someone with a narcissistic or a cynical personality. You need to engage your intellect and have the patience to observe these personality types closely. That is where it can get very tricky. People with these personality types are quick to make decisions for themselves, as well as for others. Be clear about your purpose of meeting someone and be determined to know them better before making any commitment.

You can come across such personality types while dating, in a marriage, in employee-employer relationships, business partnerships, or friendships.

Recognize narcissistic personalities

Why should you worry about recognizing a narcissist's behavior?

For those looking for short-term relationships, associating with a narcissist may not seem a big concern since many narcissistic individuals are good at impressing you in the initial meetings and will ensure that you have great time in their company. However, if you are considering a long-term relationship, you should try to know more about this personality type. It will protect you from heartbreak and mental, emotional, financial, or sexual abuse in later years.

Behavior patterns of narcissistic personalities

- ○ People with narcissistic personalities may be very good in their profession or in social gatherings, but are not good at close relationships.
- ○ They are very good at winning over those who they want to patronize. Once they have gotten someone under the control of their charm, they will start doing everything their way. They do not have much empathy for anyone. They mostly carry a feeling of entitlement with them.
- ○ They will insist that only their point of view is correct.

So, what will happen in a relationship with a narcissist?

- Your growth and well-being will not be their concern. The only thing people with these personalities care about is their self-esteem.
- They won't mind attacking your self-respect if it puts them in a better position.
- They will make you work for them with low or no return.
- They will not hesitate to insult and shame you publicly if it serves their purpose at that moment.
- They do not see any shame in cheating on you. Sometimes they will do it publicly to humiliate you; other times, they may not want you to know.

All these traits in your partner/employer/so-called friend are a recipe for a disastrous relationship.

Mutual support, mutual respect, and loving and caring feelings are critical to any healthy relationship. If these are missing, then the relationship will suffer, affecting one partner significantly more adversely. Most of the time, narcissists will never hold themselves accountable for the consequences of their actions toward others or in their own life. They just cannot accept that they can ever do anything wrong. So they will never apologize or feel sorry for their actions. On the contrary, if you want to leave them due to their behavior, they may emotionally abuse you with their gaslighting technique.

Gaslighting is the term used for manipulative behavior. The partner would first humiliate you, push you in a corner, and when you want to get out of the relationship, they will start showering love on you. This will go on in a cycle to such an extent that you will be confused about your love for the person. You will start doubting your own feelings. You will sense something is wrong in the relationship, but you may not be able to pinpoint what.

Recognizing a narcissist may be difficult in initial interactions. Their initial disposition may deceive you so much that they seem like the perfect prospect to enter into a relationship with. They may impress you with their qualities, and they may make you feel important by praising you. They will be very excited to get into a relationship with you. You may be tempted to commit to this relationship because it feels perfect. That is why you need to be cautious about someone with a narcissistic personality right in the beginning to avoid future pain.

Signs that indicate a person may have narcissistic tendencies

- **Too charming to be real** -If they are keen on getting into a relationship with you, they will be all out to impress you from the get-go and make you feel special. Nothing wrong with that. Right? Just shows how impressed they are with you. They feel something so strong for you that they are making it very clear to you that they want to have a relationship with you. The reality is that real love and affection take time to grow. If someone is being overly nice to you from the very beginning, it is a red flag. If someone comes on too strong in the initial meetings, be wary.
- **Too self-centered** -After the first red flag, you may want to observe them closely. Spend more time with them to see how they behave in others' company. Do they seem to have a real big ego? If they are always talking about themselves and their achievements, they probably are too self-centered.
- **Have no patience to listen to others** -Do they listen to others when they are expressing themselves? If they

show no interest in others or what others say and are always talking about themselves, it is something to make note of.

- **Are they feeding off others' compliments all the time?**
- If they are constantly seeking compliments from others and are always portraying themselves as the best, then they are not ever going to notice your qualities. They may pay you a compliment here and there just to keep you around to serve their purpose.
- **Extreme likes and dislikes -**
- You may notice that they don't hesitate to express extreme dislike of something or someone. Quite often, they will use derogatory words and adjectives to describe the people they dislike. They may have extreme likes also, and more often than not, they are motivated by their desire to align with someone they consider successful or likely to be helpful in fulfilling their mission. And if the status of that person changes, they may very suddenly change their opinion about them.
- **They are always critical of others** and look down upon people they think inferior to them.

I am not suggesting that you should be alarmed or avoid this person altogether if you see some of the signs of a narcissistic personality. I am also not suggesting losing out on the enjoyment of a spontaneous bond and enriching experience. The person you are interacting with may show some of those signs, but at the same time, they enrich your life and make it worthwhile.

Be aware that someone with this particular personality type takes time to show their real color. Their company may provide you an excellent honeymoon period that may last for years or for days, but eventually, their real personality traits will surface. That is when you may find yourself in the deep with no way to get to the shore.

There are many people who risk getting into relationships with narcissists because they enjoy the thrill of their company. And despite being aware of their partner's personality type, they are willing to take the risk, or they just want to believe that they could be misjudging them. Also, we sometimes like to think that the other person will change, or we will be able to change them with our love.

Hence, it would be in your best interest to assess the relationship's pros and cons and then decide whether you are willing to commit to the relationship. Either way, it is helpful to be aware of the person's personality type. This way, you will have the satisfaction of making your choice after due consideration. You will also prepare yourself to deal with the person's behavior without causing anxiety. Because of your experience, seeing some of these personality traits surfacing in the future may not hurt you as much.

Beware of pessimists

You may know them as cynics, skeptics, or pessimistic people. They are the biggest threat to a person's or society's growth. If you really want to see growth and progress in life, be it family life, your career, or in your community or the world, then you need to recognize skeptics around you and stay away from them. It may be difficult to stay away from them if they are part of your family, your team at work, or part of your buddy group. In such cases, prepare yourself to not be influenced by them because they will try very hard to make you believe that things cannot improve. At times they will even try to give you some reason as to why it can not improve.

Their reasons will be vague, such as people do not have skills, they are making up things, or it is impossible, etc. The fact is that they just cannot envision progress. They are so comfortable in the status quo that they actually fear change, or rather, they are so afraid of failure that they do not want to try doing anything that will change their circumstances. They are very averse to any kind of risk. They make it their mission to convince others to give up trying.

They will find fault with everyone and everything that is engaged in bringing about the change. And that is why it is dangerous to have them in your life, particularly if you are a risk-taker and are striving for growth. They are non-believers and will always try to attack your faith, and in the process. weaken you in your pursuits. As a result, you may not make the progress you anticipated. And then these cynics are the first to say "told you so." The fact is they will slow your progress without you even realizing it.

Now you may say, "Progress is still happening for the betterment of society."
And you know how that is possible? Because the number of believers is still larger than that of pessimistic people. The day that reverses, this world will be on a suicidal mission, on a downward trend.

It is very difficult to convert skeptics to believers. So don't waste your energy trying to change them. Just don't let them influence you. Also, make sure you don't turn into a cynic in their company.

The best way to safeguard from their negative influence is, first, to be confident of your purpose and your approach to what you are pursuing. Second, be conscious of how you react to their comments. If you let them pull your morale down, then you have let them influence you, and you do not want that. Do not let any doubt seep in and slow you down.

CHAPTER FOUR

Have Clarity about Your Intention

CLARITY PRECEDES SUCCESS

Know your purpose

For successful relationships, you need to be aware of your own intentions, and you need to be honest with yourself. Tune into your feelings to know the integrity of your intentions.

Assess what kinds of feelings you desire through this relationship.

Are you seeking mutual love and respect, or do you want to show your authority in some other way?

Are you interacting with them out of fear or some selfish intention?

Maybe you want this person around because they make you feel important and powerful.

Your intentions are pure if you are interacting with someone because you genuinely want to interact with them for their company or for the opportunity to add value to their life/ business?

ɹu are trying to get close to someone, to be their
ɹant, just to get information out of them that you can use
ne future for commercial gain or to blackmail them, then
ɹu have bad intentions. Be aware that you will have to face
the consequences of your good and bad intentions.

Are you adding value, or are you a liability?

In every relationship you need to ask yourself one question.

"Am I adding value for this person/entity? Are my intentions honest in this relationship?"

Be conscious that value does not just come with gifts and favors. You add value when you make someone happy, when you make them feel confident and secure, when in your presence, they feel at ease and want to share their feelings and experiences with you. This kind of value elevates energy levels for both parties.

If your intentions are to add value, then even if you criticize others, they will understand that you want to help them and not hurt them.

CHAPTER FIVE

Give Time to Nurture and Grow Relationships

Once you have made your relationship choices, then nurture these relationships with unconditional love. They may not be exactly as you would like them to be. At times, they may even give you some of those negative feelings that you wanted to avoid in the first place. Still, it is better to give these relationships time rather than jumping to conclusions and terminating them too quickly.

We quite often get blinded by our own preconditioning and do not have patience to give the other person a benefit of doubt, a second chance. More often than not, others are not even aware of why you were disappointed with them, because they may have been busy dealing with their own life situations or insecurities. You may lose an opportunity to have a good relationship. If you are uncertain and have questions about other's intentions, don't hesitate to have a conversation to understand their intentions better. You will need to be open-minded during these conversations and not judgmental or accusatory.

There have been a couple of instances in my life when I was so preoccupied with my own thoughts that I just did not notice someone saying "hello" to me or smiling at me, and I felt really bad about it later. Sometimes, I realized it after I had already passed them. And in some such cases, I noticed the other person's attitude toward me had changed in our next interaction. They became more cautious, or unfriendly.

It used to hurt me before my self-awakening. Not any more though. I can understand the reason for their changed attitude. But interestingly, it happened not because I had any bad intentions. It was just because they did not try to know me better. They did not give me a benefit of doubt.

Adopt a service attitude

Shift your focus from wanting to be liked and loved to what you are offering in the relationship.

> 99
>
> # You can make more friends in two months by becoming interested in other people than you can in two years by trying to get people interested in you
>
> DALE CARNEGIE
>
> 66

Once you start focusing on what you are bringing to the table, instead of focusing on what others are giving or not giving you, people will want to have you as a friend, as a co-worker, and as an employee or employer; family members will love your company. Every time you interact with others, before judging their actions, before getting irritated with them, ask yourself:

"Is my intention pure in this interaction?"

"Am I interacting without bias, without prejudgment, and with a growth mindset, with an intention of developing the relationship further, with an intention of adding value for everyone involved?"

You may say adopting a service attitude is easier said than

done. True, initially it may not seem simple as it will require you to be more aware of your thoughts, feelings, and actions, but once you get the hang of it, it will come naturally to you when you interact with others.

We all want to spend time with those who make us feel good in their company. Appreciation and compliments uplift our mood and make us feel good about ourselves. So why not pay more compliments? They should be genuine and heartfelt though. Others can feel the authenticity or fakeness of your compliments.

Sometimes you don't actually have to even say anything. If your appreciation is genuinely from the heart, you will convey the feeling through your body language. They will still know how you made them feel.

Respect and trust them for who they are

When we accept others as they are, it gives them the freedom to be their natural selves. Accepting people means their behavior does not bother us.

We all desire that others respect us for who we are. We hate it when someone underestimates our capabilities, judges us, or criticizes us. So, for good relationships, this respect needs to be mutual.

You cannot expect to be respected by someone who you do not respect, however much you may demand it. Good rapport is established when both interacting parties respect each other for who they are. You can find something worth respecting in everyone. If you cannot respect them for their most obvious personality traits, talent, knowledge, or skills, you may find qualities like purity of intention, integrity, discipline, or a hardworking attitude. You may respect them for their intent to have relationship with you.

I have seen some people, especially from affluent classes, ill-treating their subordinates, demanding the utmost respect from their domestic help, while they themselves treat their workers like slaves. They do not feel the need to respect these workers for their contributions and hard work. They behave as if they are entitled to all that respect, and they are entitled to treat their workers badly. This behavior is entirely from a desire to feed their own egos and to prove that others are less than them. Interestingly, the harder they try to extract this respect, the less likely they are to get genuine respect. Additionally, they have a perception that being nice to their subordinates spoils them.

How do they not see the qualities and contributions of their workers? They do not notice that their workers are trying their best to earn respect as well, and they also yearn for it.

People with these big-ego personalities get surprised when the same workers revolt and either leave them or take an extreme step of shaming them publicly.

This also happens in many man-woman relationships and parent-child relationships. One considers himself/herself to be above the other and demands respect. They just don't know how to earn respect. They don't realize that first they have to respect the other party. Also, in parent-child relationships, the best way to inculcate certain behavior is by example. Parents need to respect their children as much as they feel the need to be respected for their role.

In all these scenarios, the person in authority is trying to create fear and not respect. Genuine respect has got nothing to do with your knowledge, experience, status, money, or role. It is everything to do with your behavior. If you respect others, they are more likely to respect you.

Trust their decisions in whatever they have undertaken to do. Show confidence in their abilities, even if you may not agree with their choices. In joint responsibilities, either as parents or team members working on a project, everyone needs to be respected for what they bring to the table, to get the best results of combined effort. When everyone feels respected, differences of opinion can be discussed in a mature way and consensus can be achieved.

Never give unsolicited advice

There are people who will give you the impression that they have solutions for all the problems in the world. They may not be very successful at finding solutions for their own problems, or they may not even recognize their own problems, but they will be very eager to point out problems in others' lives and then provide solutions for them. These people are bound to have friction in their relationships.

You certainly do not want to have such a personality.

When you point out issues in another's life, you are implying that they are not capable of recognizing problems in their life. Second, you may be seeing something as a problem from your perspective, whereas it may not be a problem for that person from their perspective. For example, if you tell a close friend or a relative, "How can you live with a person like this? Your husband/wife is so stubborn. Or he/she is so disrespectful." Or if you tell someone "I think you should arrange your furniture like this," or "I think you should be stricter with your children," you are implying that they are not capable of recognizing a need for change. As if they were just waiting for you to open their eyes to it.

You may be better at those skills, but by giving unsolicited advice, you are indirectly looking down upon them or making them feel lacking in some way.

In my opinion, you should never give unsolicited advice. Certainly give your best advice when someone asks you for it and has already identified the need for it.

I have personally felt so let down or irritated with someone giving me unsolicited advice.

There is a wise saying -**"If you want to give light to others, first you have to glow yourself."**

Sometimes it can be quite a challenge to hold yourself back from giving advice, particularly when you see a loved one suffering, or dealing with some bad situations in their lives, such as serious disease or financial hardship. For example, if someone close to you has an addiction and is not willing to admit it, and you are worried about them; or when you have educated yourself in a certain field, such as learning about healthy foods or healthy lifestyles, and what you know could improve their health; or you may have a better understanding of managing finances, and you want to help.

It is a hard reality that even in these situations unsolicited advice does not work.

If you are genuinely concerned about the other person and want to help, the best approach would be to first put them at ease, to remove the stress of the situation. "I told you so" is the most counterproductive and hurtful expression for a person who is already feeling like failure.

Once the other person is feeling at ease and is willing to confide in you, to lean on you for support, then try to put actual solutions in front of them. Instead of telling them that they need to eat healthy, offer them the choice of healthy meals. Instead of telling them "that was the most irresponsible choice you could have made," put them in an environment that is conducive to responsible choices. Instead of scolding them for being reckless with money, teach them better money management by example. And if they are facing a dire financial crisis, just provide support by lending money, if you can, to ease the situation. Advice in such situations is not timely and does not show that you actually care. It merely seems an effort to prove yourself right.

Love, respect and trust can never be demanded. Love is just felt. It is not something to be exchanged. Respect and trust are earned. And to earn respect and trust you need to focus on your words and actions. You cannot force others to respect or trust you.

I really liked this quote that was posted by a contact on LinkedIn –
"True love is not found. It is built."

CHAPTER SIX

Managing Expectations for Yourself and for Others

Keep the guesswork out

If you are not clear of the purpose of the relationship, and you are not sure what each party is bringing in the relationship, you need to discuss it openly, instead of making guesses, and then regretting it later or feeling guilty for misjudging the other's capabilities. Expecting others to read your mind or to know about your skills is not practical and can be most frustrating.

Initially, when I joined workforce, being very shy, I would not open up or boast about my skills and talents., If someone asked me specifically about certain skills, I would respond matter-of-factly. I believed that once others saw my work they would know about my talent. Later, I realized that was not a good approach. No one, especially in the workplace, has time to get to know about your skills in due course. They all want to know about you from the get-go. And these days, with the job market being so competitive, you need to express your skills and talents very clearly upfront.

Of course, you should not lie about them, either, to get a job. Though "fake it till you make it" may work if you very desperately want a job and are willing to learn along the way. But this would also mean putting yourself on the spot every day till you get to the desired skill level. You should be prepared for the challenge, and then enjoy the process. Others will not mind as long as you deliver as expected.

If the roles are reversed and you need to make sure that someone will deliver as expected, you want to have clarity about their capability. Best practice is to have open discussions and ask questions till you get that clarity. Don't presume someone has talent or skills just because they have a certain background, or they graduated from a prestigious college or institution.

You may want to know more about what they expect to get from the relationship, what their aspirations are, and what kind of trajectory they see in their future life. Here you need to be able to discern, to the best of your ability, the fake responses from true responses. And all this should be done with an open mind and being true to yourself.

Apply a strategy of undercommitting and overdelivering

Many optimistic people set high expectations for themselves as well as for others. There's nothing wrong with that as long as they are not too optimistic to be realistic, and they do not promise anything openly. If you are very optimistic and like to set high goals to motivate you, keep these goals private. Once you achieve them, others will see the results and appreciate them much more than if you had shared them from the beginning. To put it another way, do not overcommit (to yourself or to others), as it may lead to feeling guilty for not achieving targeted goals if you fail in your endeavor. It is better to undercommit and overperform.

You can have big ambitions, but keep them to yourself. If you share them, people start expecting specific results from you. If you are not able to meet your goals, you may end up feeling guilty and doubting your ability. You should never have to feel guilty for being ambitious. It can also affect your credibility as others may start having doubts about your ability too. Inadvertently, it may become a personality trait of yours to set difficult goals that you don't strive to fulfill, and you don't mind not fulfilling them, because you have learned to accept failure. If you set right goals and have a realistic plan, you will achieve your goals and make everyone and yourself proud.

You definitely want to work toward the feeling of pride rather than feeling of guilt. Feeling guilty affects your health more than any other negative feeling. And not achieving targeted goals is not what you desire. It certainly doesn't make you feel good.

Do not keep scorecards

One big reason for the large number of divorces is because people always want each interaction in a relationship to be some kind of business dealing, where people are always calculating the give and take. They are a bit guarded lest they get hurt, and they are always analyzing the other person's actions instead of questioning and focusing on their own actions and intentions. If you desire love and affection from a spouse or partner, then you need to focus on your own loving thoughts for them and have faith that they will reciprocate. You need to identify the lovable qualities in others that attract you toward them and then focus on that.

Do not expect favors.

Do not waste a thought on expecting returns for favors or gifts, and please do not let it influence your behavior toward an individual.

Thoughts like "I gave a gift and never got one in return" should not influence your behavior toward others.

Your behavior reflects your personality, not theirs.

"I helped a lot, but it was not reciprocated. Now, I will not talk to this friend, co-worker, or family member." These thoughts show immaturity. You had a choice to give or not to give a gift, to help or not help, but you chose to support the other person. You got the satisfaction of making a good choice. Most of the time, a gesture of gifting and charity is motivated by our own need of self-validation. As mentioned earlier, such gestures make us feel good about ourselves.

Expecting something in return is not good for relationships, and it undermines the purity of your intentions. The other person will do what seems right to them. There is no point in holding it against them. They could be dealing with bigger issues in their lives, or they are not the gift-giving type. It could also be that they don't know what to get you or are not sure whether you will like it or not.

CHAPTER SEVEN

Resolving Differences

Recognize moments of friction

There are so many articles and blogs on the internet with headings like "Reasons He Doesn't Love You Anymore," "Signs that Your Marriage Is Over," and "Signs that You Are Roommates Instead of Lovers." Such articles force you to look for problems even if they don't exist. I don't understand why people have to dig for signs of unhappiness. It certainly is not good to be unhappy in a relationship, but you do not need to focus on finding that unhappiness. You will know when and why you are unhappy if a problem arises. And that will be the time to find solutions and not focus on problems.

In my opinion, all relationships will have some moments of friction. It is normal, and it makes a relationship more dynamic and realistic. As long as these moments are few and far in between and do not cause any noticeable emotional damage. Minor frictions are bound to happen because of personality differences, differences in preferences, and differences in approaches to dealing with certain life situations. These should not be cause of much concern. Friction can also happen as a result of two entities evolving or growing differently. It is helpful to recognize these instances of friction and address them in a timely manner.

Does your partner need your understanding and love?

When you notice certain changes in your relationship dynamics, it would be prudent to pause and observe—try to find the cause of friction. Notice how both of you are behaving and feeling. Is someone feeling neglected, let down, rejected, unappreciated, unloved? Or is it something else?

Signs that something is amiss when one or both parties:

- Become short-tempered and get angry easily
- Have stopped sharing and keep to themselves
- Show signs of suspicion and are always trying to confirm the other's intentions
- No longer express their love openly or are inhibited in expressing it
- Seem disengaged
- Have become more critical and blame the other for every bad situation

Any one of these signs indicates that the person behaving or feeling like this is experiencing their own internal dialogue about some situations in their life, and it is consuming quite a bit of their energy. They need support and understanding. Sometimes it could be that both partners are going through this experience due to tough life situations. Other times it could be just one person evolving differently. If both partners are experiencing this and are not able to respond to the situation with a rationale mind, then they may need external help to resolve their differences and move forward.

In the majority of instances, it could be just one party feeling like this, or one may be feeling it more than the other because of their personality types. In such instances, the other party can help ease the situation.

If you are not the one feeling dejected or low on energy, and you are serious about the relationship, then you can help by recognizing the need to do something.

In most cases, the previously mentioned behavior is a sign that this person is experiencing a lack of attention, love, or validation. It could also be that responsibilities are overwhelming them, and they are not feeling appreciated for their efforts.

If the change is out of the norm, then most likely some recent incident has caused it. You may try to find out what that could be, give extra attention to them. Try to empathize with them and be more understanding of their feelings and their situation.

It is not easy to behave positively if the other person is shouting at you and blaming you for every wrong. If you have been wanting to get out of this relationship, you may not feel motivated to do anything and may use this as an excuse to walk out. But if you made a genuine commitment to have this as a long-term relationship, then more than ever, you partner needs your support now.

And the best way to provide that support is by paying more attention, by doing things together, by spending time together, and by listening to their complaints with a calm mind instead of reacting violently or distancing yourself.

Do YOU need to express your feelings?

If you are feeling low on energy, mean, suspicious, or angry, then you need to pause and think. Acknowledge these feelings and express them to others instead of waiting for them to figure out what is bothering you. Also, it will be in your best interest to mend the situation with your partner instead of running to outsiders for support. They may make it worse by giving you wrong advice or by creating ill feelings in your mind against your partner.

If your partner stays aloof and does not engage in finding a solution, then it may be a sign that they don't really care about your feelings. If they are not very committed, then they may use your changed behavior as an excuse to get out of the relationship. This kind of reaction from a partner can be really hurtful and can make the situation worse.

You will need lots of courage and determination to find a solution to deal with this situation. In a marriage, if your partner is disengaged instead of trying to understand you, you need to rethink your marriage.

If your partner is really great in every other respect but refuses to share your feelings, then instead of trying to find someone else to lean on, to share your feelings with, the best first step would be to become emotionally self-reliant. Learn the art of enjoying your own company.

If the partnership is becoming more of a liability, you may choose to get out of it.

Also, all through this process of finding an amicable solution, it would be advisable to see things from your partner's perspective, to understand their point of view before jumping to conclusions.

Communication is the best tool in dispelling misunderstandings

Communication is the key. Everyone is not willing to communicate to sort out misunderstandings. Because they don't like conflicts, they evade discussions too. I recently heard someone say, "Communication is the fuel for a relationship." It seemed a good analogy. Ongoing communication helps each relationship move forward.

Tips to keep the communication going include:
- Remember likes, dislikes, and important dates
- Try to make a note of their likes, dislikes, birthdays, anniversaries, pets, and their favorites. All of us have a list of contacts. Make note of this additional info about your contacts. Remember to send greeting cards, thank you notes, and the occasional "How are you doing?" notes to check on them.

You may wonder why one needs to worry about such superfluous activities to show your love for others. You share a love bond with them. Shouldn't that be good enough? These little gestures also make us spend time thinking about relationships that matter to us. And similarly, it makes the recipient feel good, knowing that you thought of them and you care about them.

Dale Carnegie, in his book How to influence People and Make Friends, makes a point that people love it when others remember little details about them. Successful salesmen use it effectively to impress their prospects, and many leaders have won the hearts of their followers by remembering their names or important dates in their lives and by sending them little notes of appreciation.

Assign some time to communicate periodically
Keeping communication channels open keeps you tuned into others. It is an indicator that these relationships matter to

you, and you want to stay in touch. You want to know what is going on in their lives. You want to feel their feelings and provide support if required.

Be fully engaged

Current information overload is making people behave in a very distracted way most of the time. People are trying to multitask and end up being less engaged in their interactions. For example, your spouse is telling you about a situation at work and you are too engaged in a TV program to understand much of what your spouse is trying to convey. How can you help your spouse if he/she needs your advice when you did not find it important enough to even engage yourself fully in the conversation?

Give them a chance to express themselves

A healthy two-way communication is when both parties are good at listening.

Don't be in a rush to comment negatively on their thoughts, decisions, or actions, even if you disagree. Jumping to conclusions in haste and reacting to what others do or say instantly is detrimental to relationships. Pause to process the situation and then respond. Develop the skill to respond and not react to situations.

Hear them out and then express yourself. Before you say something hurtful to others, always think how you would feel if someone said the same thing to you.

Sometimes, people intentionally say bad things to hurt the other person. This, however, is not a sensible strategy, as it does not resolve the issue. Rather, it aggravates the matter further.

Respond, do not react

Think before you react to others' words and actions.

When you feel that you are being insulted or disrespected by someone, do recognize it, but do not react with negative emotions, such as anger, revenge, sadness, or guilt. Instead, realize that their behavior is either due to their inability to resolve issues amicably, or due to their own insecurities.

You may have had an experience of your spouse, friend, colleague, or boss becoming angry with you when you said or did something. And like most people in such situations, you may have counterattacked or tried to defend yourself.

Quite often, verbal exchanges in such situations go on for quite some time till one person decides to leave in anger or frustration and a whole lot of bitterness. Most of the time, this leads to a feeling of guilt for one party or for both, and all this results in an unnecessary drainage of energy without any positive resolution.

Dealing with someone's anger is challenging. However, the best approach would be to not react instantly. Rather, take time to process the situation, to understand where they were coming from: their perspective, their personality, or their insecurities. Do not try to defend yourself. It will make you feel worse. Process every aspect of the situation and then respond.

Responding, while technically also a reaction, takes into consideration the desired outcome of the interaction. The outcome of a reaction is accidental—it could be positive or negative—whereas a response is engineered to produce a specific positive outcome. Reacting is emotional and responding is intentional.

Do not let criticism affect you

Do not take it to heart when someone criticizes you. If you are confident of your abilities, you should not mind how others judge you. They judge only from their perspective, which, in a given situation, is probably different from yours. How about adopting this attitude of Mahatma Gandhi?

"Nobody can hurt me without my permission."

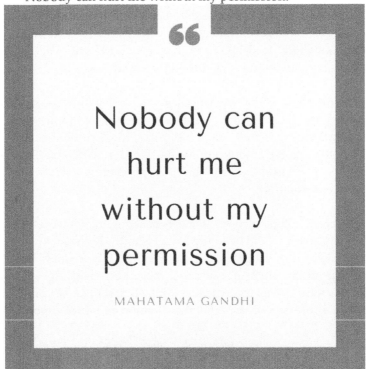

Nobody can hurt me without my permission

MAHATAMA GANDHI

Try to understand others' perspectives

When asked
"What is the reason
for every
misunderstanding?"
Swami Vivekananda answered
"The reason is –
we see other people
as we are, but not as
they are"

It helps to see things from another person's perspective. Putting ourselves in their position can help us be more empathetic and compassionate.

CHAPTER EIGHT

Accept Others as They are

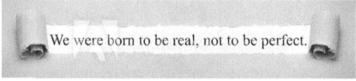

We were born to be real, not to be perfect.

When a photographer cannot change a scene, he changes his lens or angle to capture the best of that scene. Similarly, if we cannot change a situation or a person, we need to change our perspective to recognize the best they have to offer.

If there are too many differences that cannot be sorted out with communication, then trying to push someone to change is not going to work. It will be a frustrating uphill task. Especially if, in your mind, you are always blaming the other person for your unhappiness. And if your intentions are to please your own ego by telling others that there is something wrong with them and they are not worthy of your company, then you are to be blamed for the messed-up relationship. You will need to change yourself.

If you desire a well-balanced and healthy relationship, then you need to accept others as they are.

There is a wise saying: "If you don't like something, change it. If you cannot change it, then accept it." In relationships make a choice—a choice to accept the other person as they are (if they play a significant role in your life as a sibling, spouse, friend, in-law, or employer) or to terminate the relationship.

If you choose to accept them as they are, along with their baggage of preconditioning and their personality traits that come with it, then this acceptance has to be with a feeling of submission and not resistance. Be conscious that you made a choice to accept the other person as they are because you value this relationship, and you want to continue the relationship in a healthy way. If done with full awareness of the involved compromises, quite often, negative feelings go away with just this act of acceptance.

CHAPTER NINE

Social Media and Relationships

Enrich relationships with intuitive personal interactions rather than communicating through social media. When you communicate everything to a large group where is the one-to-one interaction? How can you form real bonds through mass communication?

People are spending so much time on mass communication that they are ignoring those who are close to them physically.

I have never understood the relevance of a person wishing their spouse a "Happy Anniversary" or "Happy Birthday" on social media. When in-person communication is possible and the message is very personal, why do people post it on social media? I personally do not like being wished happy birthday on social media, especially if I am next to the person, or I'm accessible through one-to-one media, such as a phone call or a text.

It seems like everyone has suddenly become a celebrity and is so busy that they do not have time to greet their loved ones in person.

And if they are posting on social media in addition to the in-person greeting, what purpose is that serving? Are they trying to tell the rest of the world how much they love their spouse or family member? Or is it that their loved ones won't believe them without a public display of their affection? I see it more as an effort to serve their own ego by showing the world how caring they are.

I have yet to find out if it has helped strengthen relationships in any way.

CHAPTER TEN

Be Determined to Have a Positive Outcome

Be determined to have a positive outcome from each interaction in a relationship. Do not let fear of failure in a personal or professional relationship influence your thinking to such an extent that you yourself cause your relationships to fail you.

To elaborate, let's say you want a job really badly and you want to start a new professional relationship. You start preparing for the job interview. The outcome of the interview will depend quite a bit on what kind of outcome you were expecting. You cannot say, "If I am lucky, I will get it." Also, while preparing for the interview, if you are having an internal dialogue, like "What will happen if I don't get the job? I won't have money to pay my bills. There are so many qualified candidates. I don't think I have much chance," then you certainly are not assured a positive outcome.

Books are full of examples of people winning by sheer belief in themselves and their efforts. All successful people believe in a positive outcome, even if it means first facing a few failures.

Be conscious that you always have a choice

In addition to being aware of your feelings, words, and

actions at the time of interaction, you also need to be aware that you always had a choice when you started the relationship or conversation, and you also have a choice to terminate it if it does not align with your life's purpose.

It would not be fair to you or the other person to stay in the relationship with resistance or friction for the rest of your life.

CHAPTER ELEVEN

You and Only You Make the Choices for Your Life

You also have the choice to make it clear to the other person that you do not like certain things about their behavior and you will not tolerate them. They need to either accept your terms to continue the relationship or terminate it. If they are difficult and will never listen or change, and you are not able to accept their behavior because it bothers you tremendously and affects your day-to-day life, then it is best to leave the relationship altogether.

You will always have these choices, but you should also be willing to accept the consequences of the choices you make. Sometimes, the consequences of these choices seem so scary that you tend to defer making a choice. Well, there are consequences –if you don't make a choice too. You stay in a state of status quo, which could be one of suffering, unhappiness, sadness, and dejection.

Over time, you may learn to accept your situation, as well as accept others as they are, and then live happily. If you are willing to adjust your expectations and not expect others to match your standards in every respect, you may see yourself liking them more.

"When you stop expecting people to be perfect, you can like them for who they are." – Donald Miller

Part-2

Relationship in a Marriage

Other than parent-child and sibling relationships, there are two types of personal relationships that one invests in quite a bit—life partners and friends.

CHAPTER TWELVE

Start it Right by Picking The Right Partner

What is a spouse, or life partner?

The dictionary defines a spouse as either member of a married pair in relation to the other; one's husband or wife. If you check the meaning of marriage, you get this: any of the diverse forms of interpersonal union established in various parts of the world to form a familial bond that is recognized legally, religiously, or socially, granting the participating partners mutual conjugal rights and responsibilities.

Another definition: a relationship in which two people have pledged themselves to each other in the manner of a husband and wife.

Marriage is the longest and strongest bond one can form outside of blood relations. Like with most other relationships, it does demand some compromises and adjustments, again because each one of us is preconditioned to quite an extent by our upbringing long before we find our marriage partner.

Additionally, this is one relationship where you end up

sharing space so closely.

Before tying the knot for a long-term commitment, you need to be aware that you are doing this from your own choice, and not under any external influence.

Be well aware that if a marriage, on one hand, offers companionship, love, security, and family life. It also demands a full commitment from the heart. This commitment entails dealing with certain challenges that come with sharing space, time, thoughts, responsibilities, and other material assets with someone.

In these close relationships, with so much sharing, we combine our energies and make it a shared power. One tends to influence the other's choices of their career, what they should experience together, what information they should consume, what they should watch for entertainment, what they should read, what they should eat, where they should travel together, and who they should socialize with.

Picking the right partner

Though love at first sight, and childhood infatuations often lead to marriages; when you are consciously searching for a partner through dating sites, at events, and in social gatherings, it can be helpful to have clarity on what type of person you are looking for.

At the same time, following the general rules of relationships will make it easier. Check your feelings toward the person and try to feel their intentions. Is he/she genuinely seeking a companion for keeps, and do they understand what that means? Is he/she determined to tie the knot solely on the basis of pure love? Or is one of you in it because of some other selfish intention, such as conquering someone, obtaining higher status, having more money, or experiencing sexual satisfaction? You can find many examples of such marriages where these intentions have played a role, from one or both the partners. These marriages end up failing, or they become marriages of convenience.

When intentions are pure from both partners, then it can be a lifelong honeymoon, and the world can seem like heaven.

Life will throw many kinds of challenges your way— financial hardships, separations because of jobs, disagreements on many matters (children's upbringing, financial matters, lifestyle), which are mostly because of differences in your respective partner's upbringing and general personality traits. But as long as your relationship is based on pure love, all those can be sorted out.

Recognize intention – true or motivated

It can be difficult to tell the difference between pure intention and motivated intention. If there is an ulterior motive other than companionship that encourages a person to get into a relationship, then it is a motivated intention. If someone has learned the tricks to say nice things even when they don't sincerely mean them, or improve appearances to look attractive, or sexy so that they could win you over or seduce you, then they may have motivated intentions.

Dealing with similarities and differences

The saying– "opposites attract" does sound interesting and may seem romantic, but there is also a logic to it. Each one of us has strengths and weaknesses, or personality traits that we admire in others but just don't have in our personalities. Sometimes, we wish to be like others. That's when we are attracted to "the opposite."

A relationship with people who have opposite characteristics will work only if both people are aware of the differences and use them as something that complements their own personalities. They may get a sense of completeness in the company of the other person who has a different personality.

You do not have to have the same perspective on everything, and the same preference of interaction with the outside world, as long as you acknowledge, accept, and respect each other's preferences. And once you recognize and accept these differences, you should provide unconditional support to your partner's choices. This way you will help each other grow and increase your cumulative power.

Feel beautiful

People will always see you from their perspective and through the filter of their conditioning. You can't force them to see you differently. It is critical that your spouse, or partner, likes you for who you are, and that their feelings are not based on misconceptions.

Trying to look different to please someone or win someone over will not lead to a long-lasting relationship. If it is very important to you that others approve of your appearance, then you may have to make an effort to look or act differently to be noticed. For example, if you don't feel comfortable in a miniskirt but you think you will get noticed if you wear miniskirts, then you are hiding your real self.

You can try to show off your changed look, and then just wish and hope that you get noticed. There is no guarantee that others will notice you, because not everyone has the same perspective, and you interact with so many people.

How many times will you change yourself to impress others? So much effort for what? You cannot control or change others' perceptions. You can only control what you feel and do.

Why not just look and act in ways that are comfortable, feel good about yourself, and be confident that people will respect you for your individual style? Don't waste your time trying to impress others. Be proud of your looks and exude confidence in your appearance.

Driving habits can tell quite a bit about personalities

Observing someone's driving style can help identify their personality type.

Say I do not care about the look and color of a car, as long as it drives well and serves its purpose. I am a slow and cautious driver who likes to listen to country music while I am driving. I do not mind arriving a bit late at my destination because I want to reach there safely, without causing myself much stress.

There is another person who likes to own expensive, flashy cars and drive fast and who gets a kick when other drivers notice him and his car on the road. He takes chances with speed bumps by not slowing down. He may also be someone who derives great pleasure if, on a muddy road, his car splashes dirt on passersby. And other drivers, though in awe of this car, have to roll up their windows to avoid the dirt. He may get angry if someone else tries to pass him and he is impatient at a red light.

These characteristics, in a very subtle way, serve as a mirror to our personalities. They can tell us if the driver has a big ego, is a show-off, or if that person is humble and likes to keep a low profile, has compassion and understanding for others, or is on his own trip all the time. Whether that person is cautious while making decisions or has an impulsive personality; whether that person is calm or is stressed in difficult situations.

You have to understand the personality of the person you are dealing with and then make your choice to accept or not accept them for who they are.

Now, in a marriage, it could be that both partners are cautious drivers. There is a likelihood of less friction in their relationship, but it could also become boring at times.

If they both like flashy cars and drive aggressively, there will be a lot of excitement, but chances of accidents will always loom. There may be friction over who will drive the car or have control in the marriage. If not addressed with understanding, this can become serious and cause friction.

And then there is another combination, where one partner takes the safer route and the other flies down the muddy road, or the one where both partners have a compatible combination of these personality traits.

This example is just one illustration of how to learn about another person's personality traits. In general, spending a good amount of time with another person in various situations will give you a better understanding of their personality type.

Life can be pleasure to live if both partners recognize their personality types, and accept each other as they are without judging. They do not try to change each other and believe in seeing the positive side of these personality traits.

CLARITY PRECEDES SUCCESS

Clarity on the purpose of marriage

It is good to be clear why you have decided to marry someone.

Most of the time, after a few dates, one or both individuals start visualizing how it would be if they got to spend more time together. For those who enjoy their sexual compatibility, it would be the excitement of having more time for it. The majority of dating couples are seeking this satisfaction because of their active hormones, because of their body's innate desire. In some cases, for those who don't like the loneliness of being single, it would mean having someone around to help dispel the loneliness.

If you find this analysis dry, then let's talk of romance. In my opinion, so-called "romance" is a creation of our imagination, mainly inspired by romantic stories in novels and movies. We are able to generate feelings of love and passion by thinking of someone in a certain way. Spouses are able to keep this feeling of romance in their marriage by thinking of their partner with passion, by saying loving things, and by doing things that would please their partner.

The love at first sight, as mentioned earlier, can be quite true because of the attraction between two spiritual energies, because of their harmonic vibrations. And more often than not, physical attractions or infatuations also happen due to some such interaction, also known as a quantum moment. Those who find love this way and then decide to get married are really lucky.

Interestingly, quantum moments have nothing to do with anyone's marital status. They can happen anywhere, with anyone.

It is not necessary for a marriage to be a result of such a quantum moment. If everyone kept waiting for such a moment in their life, they may get old in the process and may never get married.

Marriage is more of a practical arrangement, which has been in our society for centuries, and keeps it orderly and less chaotic. Though, of course, as mentioned earlier, it is mutual love, respect, and understanding that make a marriage work.

Most of the time, two individuals who like each other's company and find the other acceptable as per their perceptions of a good life partner decide to tie the knot at a time when they are eager to procreate and become husband and wife. They may or may not give any thought to how they will bring up kids together, how they will spend time together, how they will manage their finances, and how they will deal with difficult situations in life. This is the basic truth of a married life.

Very rarely, two individuals, engaged to be married, discuss these things. They may discuss what kind of wedding they will have, where they will go for a honeymoon, what places they will travel to, and so on. It certainly is not very romantic to discuss unforeseen future issues, but those are the real issues of a married life. So it would be prudent to get to know other person's thoughts on real-life issues.

Married life is full of responsibilities, and it can be enjoyable if both partners understand their responsibilities and are determined to do their best to meet them.

In many societies, where marriages are arranged, the marital focus is mainly to procreate, to grow the family tree. In most instances, these marriages have the potential of being successful because partners enter this partnership with an open mind, knowing that they chose that person mainly due to their suitability based on some preset standards, such as earning capacity, family status, cultural background, or looks. Beyond that, if, after spending some time together, they feel that they like each other's company, they say yes to the arrangement.

CHAPTER THIRTEEN

Tied The Knot, Now What?

Once two individuals commit to spending the rest of their lives with each other, just the thought of marriage creates happy emotions in them because it seems a promise of shared experiences, of cheerful moments, of creating a life together in the coming years.

When you decide to marry someone, this commitment brings you so much happiness and joy that any other happy experience of the past seems to pale in comparison. That is because marriage holds a promise of a lifetime of happiness. You don't even realize when you gradually start giving so much importance to this other person's presence in your life that your emotional state is dependent on them. You start believing that this person makes you happy.

You should feel happy, but you should also be conscious to keep the key to your happiness in your own hands. Do not let your happiness depend on others. Your happiness is in your very personal emotion vault. No one else should be able to open or control it.

You made the choice to allow yourself to open up, to share

your love, to commit to someone whom you feel extremely connected to. That is nice and helpful to live a fulfilling life. However, nobody can make us happy or unhappy.

If you're feeling happy because you found a great partner, a great companion, spouse, or lover, it is because you have chosen to bring that happy feeling to yourself.

It is our reaction to situations that makes us happy or unhappy.

There are individuals who sometimes end up making a commitment to a marriage, without being fully committed to it in their mind. This could be because of some pressure from their family, or some pressure from the person they are supposed to marry. They are likely to have doubts about the success of this marriage. That means they have already created a feeling of unhappiness associated with the alliance. They are very likely to have many unhappy moments in their marriage, unless they are aware that they can still retain control of their personal happiness. It is in their hands to leverage the alliance to grow that happiness.

Give the relationship time to blossom

Once you have made the choice of establishing a long-term relationship, always give yourself time to build confidence and trust in the new relationship. Don't rush to doubt your partner's intentions.

LET THE LOVE FLOW

Marriage allows two individuals to feel connected by being in close physical proximity; two individuals become a big part of each other's daily creation of perceptions; they knowingly or unknowingly start to influence each other's habits, mannerisms, and decision-making.

This relationship can be a relationship of growth if partners have positive expectations. They expect to grow to be better individuals in each other's company; they expect to learn from other and want to learn and explore the world together; they expect to support their spouse and are confident of being supported in difficult times. Generating these feelings is in an individual's own hands.

This will give positive energy for the relationship to grow in the right direction. Doubts should have no place in the mindset of growth and harmony.

Sharing close space

In marriage, people share living space, they eat together, they participate in certain activities together, and they make social appearances together.

If all this is not done with a feeling of love, trust, and respect, then united growth and marital success is in danger.

It is prudent for newlyweds to have a clear idea of what kind of living space they envision for themselves. Do their respective visions match? They can always work on small gaps. But if the gaps are large, such as one partner being OK with a two-bedroom minimalistic space, as long as it is practical, and the other associating success with having a big mansion, then there is a big gap in their expectation of their living space. Similarly, their ideas of decorating these spaces may differ.

You should not let such differences bother you. They can be sorted out by having open discussions and adapting to each other's preferences if they seem rationale and not too far from your taste. Egos should not interfere during these discussions. "My idea is better than yours" will only start fights and create friction. It will not provide any conclusive decisions.

Forming a joint routine and adjusting to another's habits

Everyone does not go to bed and wake up at the same time, have their meals at the same time, or work out at the same time. Some are light sleepers, and some are deep sleepers. Some snore in bed, and others cannot sleep because of that. After marriage, people try to follow a common routine for these basic activities. They either know or presume that their spouse likes the same kinds of food as they do and has similar wake-up or bedtime routines.

Love is when the other person's happiness is more important than your own.

H. Jackson Brown, Jr.

These joint activities create familiarity and deepen the bond. At the same time, there can be subtle differences in these patterns that may not bother you so much in beginning, but may start irritating you as time progresses. Learn to not let these little differences bother you if you want to keep the harmony in marriage and keep your love growing. The best way to do this is to remind yourself every day of the joy your partner's company brings you and be grateful for it.

Aligning with conventional husband and wife roles

In a conventional society, much before two individuals get married, they create an image of what their spouse is going to be like as a husband or as a wife. This image is quite often influenced by the relationship of their parents, or by the depiction of husband-wife roles in their culture and literature. They already have a perception of what a husband is supposed to do and what a wife is supposed to be.

In most societies, many still believe that the husband goes out to make money and the wife stays at home to take care of kids; the wife has to look pretty to keep her husband hooked. The husband is supposed to compliment the wife on her cooking and her looks every now and then, and the wife should appreciate her husband's professional success. It is also in the back of some women's mind that men have a roving eye, and some men expect their wives to start nagging a few years into their marriages. In evolving society these roles are getting blurred, particularly if marriage partners belong to the same sex.

In conventional marriages, if things do not happen as per these predefined roles and perceptions, for example if the wife is not good at cooking but is doing very well in her career, or the husband loves to cook but does not care about his financial status, then it may seem to be going against their expectations. This may create friction between the otherwise happy couple, despite them having a great love life.

If you have worked on making yourself emotionally strong, as suggested in chapter one, you have trained yourself to accept others as they are, and you have learned to adapt to changing situations, you will be able to face these surprises or expectation gaps with less resistance and avoid feeling hurt.

Stand on common ground

In marriage, two individuals decide to be united as one. A couple should pay great attention to the meaning of this union. This union is of two energies, which come from different backgrounds and upbringings; they may have different vibrational energies too. Since all energies are in motion and are on a journey, after union, two energies choose to be on a common journey, toward a common goal. So initially, for all newlyweds, in addition to enjoying their honeymoon bliss, which is entirely happening due to chemical harmony and physical attraction, it would be prudent to understand the union of energies and the alignment of goals.

Henceforth, they should consider themselves as one energy, moving toward a common goal. Personality traits and habits may differ. As long as their intentions are to grow together and to adopt a growth mindset, this marriage will be a success.

A spouse is called the better half for a reason. Spouses complement each other. Marriage unites two entities and makes them one. They become stronger and grow well together by becoming one energy.

Engage in common activities

In addition to spending time together at home, you and your spouse may be lucky to be spending your work hours close to each other if you work in the same office. Or on the contrary, you could spend even less time with your spouse if one of you has to be away for work. If you fall in the second category, make every effort to spend quality time with your spouse when at home.

Engaging in activities of common interest will help keep your bond strong. A walk in the woods, going to the gym, a common sport, going to the theater, or dining out are great ways to spend time together talking about things and sharing your thoughts. If a couple tends to spend their time doing their own respective things, in their own corners, without interacting much with each other, they may be growing in different directions and may gradually drift apart.

Accept in-laws with open arms

It is not so much due to personality differences that many people don't easily accept their in-laws as much as it is due to society's narrative about these relations. Since these relationships provide good elements of conflict in stories, storytellers have exploited them and have highlighted in-law conflict as something that is normal.

If you are smart, do not let such narratives influence you. The emphasis in every relationship should be on the individual, and not the title of the relationship.

My mother and grandmother had the most beautiful relationship I have ever seen of a mother-in-law and daughter-in-law. Living in a joint family, they would joke and laugh together, work as a team, and encourage and support each other in every respect. They interacted more like friends.

I have to admit that their situation was slightly different. I lost my father when I was five, and my mother moved in with her in-laws at their insistence. My siblings and I were brought up by our mother and by our father's parents in a joint family.

It was an environment filled with love. No relationship conflicts whatsoever.

After I got married, I personally did not experience these relationships as my husband's parents had passed away before we got married. We both regretted not having had the opportunity of spending time with them. However, I do have very close relationships (with lots of affection and caring) with my sisters-in-law, brothers in-law, and their children, and we have never had any misunderstandings or conflicts. My husband also won over my family members by having the genuine intention of sharing love. No conflicts whatsoever.

Many young couples experience some challenges with in-law dynamics, especially in the beginning, and they have to find their own way of handling these dynamics.

Quite often, the new wife may feel that the husband's mother is like the "other woman,", and the new husband may feel that his wife is too attached to, and in awe of, her own father. At times, it may make him jealous. Her father becomes the "other man."

In such situations, both partners need to make the resolution in their own hearts to not let these feelings creep into their marriage. They need to make clear that their love for each other is their top priority and that their love for their parents is natural and should never be treated like a threat to their relationship.

Resolve to always stand united and to never complain about each other to your respective parents.

Also, be more tolerant and considerate toward your in-laws because everyone has insecurities and apprehensions about being accepted. Be open-minded and accept them as they are, without trying to change them. Make the other party feel more at ease and loved, rather than feeling judged.

Also acknowledge that if they are being too indulgent with your children, it is just out of love and not to make you feel bad as a parent. Consider yourself lucky that you and your children have them in your life. And their indulgence with your children will never spoil your children or make them undisciplined. The feeling of being loved is good for your children's growth.

Resolving differences

Communication is the key in resolving differences. Communicate as often and as much as you can to share your thoughts and feelings. Don't hold them back. Be it your spouse or your in-laws, be honest and willing to express your feelings.

If you feel hurt with what they said or did, express it without making it a blame game. Make an honest, matter-of-fact statement without trying to judge their words or actions. And also express clearly why you got that feeling and what was your thought behind it.

You may again try to be introspective and check your own insecurities before discussing it. Maybe you felt hurt because you gave their words and action more thought than they deserved. It is best to give them the benefit of the doubt, at least the first time. Maybe they said it in a different context than what you thought it to be. Maybe they did not know how to behave in the given circumstance. Try to gauge their intent. Were they really trying to be hurtful, or was it an unintentional goof-up?

How you respond can bring you closer or push you apart

Clear communication in relationships is not easy. There are

many factors that influence how we communicate:
- Our upbringing
- Personality differences
- Gender
- Communication skills

Be intentional about finding time to communicate. Procrastinating and not addressing the issue is detrimental to the relationship, though sometimes it is worth pausing to confirm whether the disturbing issue is a real one. Sometimes, in a rage, you can make a mountain out of a molehill. In such instances, it is best to laugh it off and let it pass, at least the first time. If it happens repeatedly and bothers you, you may want to talk it out.

Win people gently and tactfully to your way of thinking. Few people like to be told the truth if it reflects on their judgment. So don't rush to tell what you believe to be the truth if it is likely to hurt someone's sentiments and feelings.

Don't make them feel guilty for their behavior. It does no good to anyone.

Sometimes when partners are angry or unhappy with each other's behavior, they don't mind pulling the other person down to show their anger. Or they call out their partner as the cause of their wrong action. An example would be a man telling his golf buddies that he could not make it to the game on time because his girlfriend was creating a scene.

Here is another illustration of how a spouse doesn't mind putting the blame of things going wrong on her partner just to make him feel guilty. Sandra, generally a very friendly, kind, and caring person, had a slightly demanding relationship with her husband. She always seemed to put the accountability of their wrong decisions on her husband. She never wanted to contribute to the decision-making process, even when her husband would ask for her opinion, but she would always comment negatively on the outcome. It seemed as if she was waiting for her husband to make a wrong decision so that she could put the blame on him. She seemed to get pleasure from making her husband feel guilty.

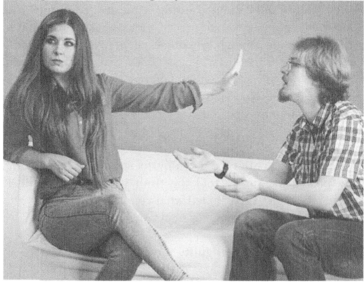

Sandra never realized that her ego was in the way of a healthy relationship with her husband. She was always trying to prove to herself that she was a devoted wife by keeping the house organized and by cooking good food for the family. She always took great pride in her role as a wife. However, she always seemed to be looking for an opportunity to pull her husband down for not doing things right.

We all know when we look at something under a microscope, it looks bigger than it is. Similarly, if we start analyzing others' personalities and habits, that too with a hidden agenda of finding faults, we will find many that would look big.

At times we need to back up and see things from a wider view. Then we will realize that those personality traits are ignorable in the bigger context.

World-renowned psychologist Dr. Paul Ekman advises that one should not let contempt seep into a relationship. Basic notion of contempt is "I am better than you and you are lesser than me. " Contempt is often accompanied by anger or a mild form of annoyance.

A healthy marital relationship is where partners support each other, are equal in decision-making, and take joint responsibility for each outcome. There should not be "me" versus "you."

In difficult times instead of complaining one should try to focus on finding a solution together. Change is easier to achieve with team effort.

In team sports players are trained to never point a finger at another player for a bad performance. It is always a combined team performance that counts.

Pulling your spouse down is likely to push you apart

If you want your partner to get ready in time for an event, then help them with some chores to make it happen instead of shouting at them to get ready fast or telling them that because of them you always reach late at events.

"You are always getting us late" is a very discouraging statement and will never get the desired result.

You, as a partner, should be willing to share the accountability for things going wrong. Sometimes it may even benefit you if you try to cover up for your partner's mistakes.

Firstly, it would make you feel good about yourself. Secondly, your partner will respect you for your gesture.

Researcher and clinician, John Gottman, has studied how contempt in marriages can signal serious relational issues. According to his research, it is the most likely to lead a marriage to a divorce if left unaddressed.

Discussions, not arguments

You may be able to win an argument by raising your voice or by insisting on your point of view, but you won't be able to change your partner's mind.

On the other hand, if you change an argument to a discussion, you bring yourself to the same level as your spouse, with an open mind. If you are willing to understand the other person's perspective, you are more likely to find a real solution, and at times, have your perspective understood better by the other person. Arguments happen because of egos, not from a desire to find solutions. Only calm discussions can help find solutions.

Never say negative things to others, even jokingly, because they cause pain that can stay in the subconscious forever.

Don't challenge others for their decisions. No one is wrong.

Humor yourself

Use humor to lighten up the tense moments. My husband has always used it effectively and made me feel at ease in difficult situations.

There is a common saying, "Don't take yourself too seriously. No one else does."

Humor helps suppress feelings of anger, resentment, and frustration.

No one wants a relationship that is serious all the time. Most of us want to be in the company of a person with whom we can laugh and be silly.

Humor helps keep the spark alive. When candlelight dinners and romantic outings don't happen as often, it is the humor in the companionship that works as the uplifter and stressbuster.

Accept your mistakes

Don't let your ego get in the way of forming a strong bond. If you think you did or said something that you shouldn't have, then don't hesitate to apologize.

Laughing together is good, but sometimes laughing at your own stupidity shows your vulnerability and strength and makes you more lovable.

Those who can laugh at themselves and, in the process, make others laugh have a special talent.

Keep guilt away

Don't ever feel guilty about past events. Don't make your partner feel guilty about their past behavior or past events either. Nagging never brings positive results to the situation. On the contrary, it only brings further aggravation and frustration. It is a big energy-drainer.

KEEP GUILT OUT OF THE WAY

Be in the present

It is difficult to control your thoughts to such an extent that you don't think of the past at all. Many situations and incidents remind you of past experiences, good or bad.

However, there is a problem if you let these memories of the past, especially of bad experiences, influence your behavior in the present.

It is not prudent to ill-treat, disrespect, or mistrust someone in the present based on your judgment of their actions of the past. People learn and change. You need to see them with fresh eyes in the present.

Sometimes, it can be thrilling and exciting to behave as if you are meeting everyone for the first time. I have trained myself to do it very consciously at times, and it creates the curiosity and excitement of a child. A child's excitement is so endearing because it lacks all judgment. Every day would seem like a new romance with your partner if you pretended that you had just met. The curiosity to know more about each other will be alive, and the hope for a great partnership in the future will excite you.

Give benefit of doubt

"He loves me. He loves me not" doubts appear in a relationship when you let suspicions enter your thoughts. As mentioned earlier, sometimes these suspicions can be entirely a result of your own imagination. In some instances, they can appear because of lack of communication or due to insecurities that you are carrying with you from your early years. For example, if you are not confident of your looks, and you think it is natural for your spouse to be attracted to someone who, in your opinion, is better looking than you, then you are most likely to ruin the relationship by doubting your partner's intentions.

Unless you have solid evidence that proves that your partner has betrayed your trust or has intentionally hurt you, you should not let any kind of suspicion affect your relationship. You should keep thoughts that create doubt and affect the marital bond at bay.

Offer space to grow

When you find someone to connect with and to share your love with, you gradually start seeing their presence as the source of your happiness. And they also depend on you to feel happiness.

You become dependent on each other and create an environment of codependency.

Over time, this codependency can turn into possessiveness, and partners behave like they are entitled to the other person's loyalty and good behavior without ever realizing that they may not be doing their part to foster a positive relationship.

With possessive behavior, one partner may mistrust the other, and the other partner may start feeling stifled. This can create a rift in the relationship, and in extreme cases, a desire to get out.

If you think your partner is being possessive and behaves as if they are entitled to your love and attention without caring for your desires, you need to express clearly to your partner that you also have expectations, and you have a right to do things and make decisions as an individual.

Any relationship where a person feels loved is difficult to disconnect from. For example, if you are living with a narcissistic person who lowers your self-esteem and belittles you in front of others, but still displays lots of love and affection for you in private just to keep you on his side as one of his admirers, it will be difficult for you to get out of this relationship. If your needs are not met and your partner does not care, it is a sign that your partner is not invested in your happiness.

Partners should watch for signs of codependency traps and try to do things that give them a feeling of freedom.

CHAPTER FOURTEEN

Change is Inevitable

Do not get into a victim mindset

The victim syndrome is defined as a condition in which a person uses their suffering, self-sacrifice, and their role as a victim to manipulate others into psychologically rewarding them for their ongoing misery.

People suffering from this syndrome think that other people are not being fair to them.

The problem is not that other people are doing certain things wrong or are doing bad things to these so-called "victims." The problem with people suffering from victim syndrome is that they themselves are not taking action to change a situation. These are people who will use all their energy to put blame on another person and declare themselves victims.

They have no intention, motivation, or energy to change the situation. They find satisfaction by proving themselves victims of a bigger conspiracy, or stronger power.

There is always a solution to a bad situation. These so-called victims, first and foremost, need to shelve the notion that they are victims. They need to change their identity from a victim to a problem solver. They can acknowledge that a given situation is not in their favor. That means they should accept the reality of the situation as a problem, and then accept that they have been assigned to solve it. They need to focus on finding the solution and take it as a mission, totally ignoring the thought that someone victimized them.

Quite often, your own lack of confidence, skills, motivation, clear purpose, pure intention, determination, and focus makes you feel like a victim of circumstances and comes in the way of you getting to a better state, experiencing a certain integrity in your relationships, or achieving a certain social status. You get in the way of your own freedom and progress when you fall prey to "victim syndrome."

If happiness is still playing hide-and-seek, pause and think like I did when I was going through a phase in my life when I hated many people. Now, the word "hate" does not exist in my dictionary. Not because I want to deny the existence of the feeling of hate. It is just that I have learned to recognize my thoughts and feelings and learned to train myself so that they don't affect me negatively.

Since I have trained myself to nurture the feeling of love more than any other negative feelings, these negative feelings hardly have room to show up. And even if they do show up accidentally, they don't stay for long, because I don't welcome them.

Unbearable differences

It can happen: you are happily married; you have a beautiful relationship; you've adapted to each other's ways. Then life that seemed like bliss initially suddenly seems to be falling apart.

It could be because you have grown apart due to external influences or different growth patterns. Maybe you made different choices along the way, or you weren't honest with yourself or with each other when you began the relationship. Quite often, your expectations for yourself and your life partner have changed, and many things that did not irritate you suddenly make you unhappy.

You feel dissatisfied with your life, or you notice this feeling that has been developing over some time. What do you do?

You have two choices:

Choice 1 – Look inward like I did. Introspection will help you identify the reason for your unhappiness. Is it really your partner, or is it you who has changed? Visualize your life going forward. How would it look like if you stayed together, and how would it be if you separated?

And if, upon introspection, you feel that it was life that, somewhere along the way, overwhelmed you and caused a rift in your relationship, then there is hope.

Upon introspection, if you feel you have changed, and if you corrected it, life would get better, then you know what to do.

If you think you both are overwhelmed (because of the day-to-day demands of life: work, finances, taking care of children), then you just need to accept that, and take action to correct it and deal with it as partners. Sometimes one partner may not be keen on acknowledging or talking about these issues. In such situations, you need to take the initial step of starting the discussion to figure out a plan. There can be resistance from your partner, but the problem will need to be addressed.

Communication is the key to resolving such issues. Working together as a team allows you to face big challenges in life and come out stronger on the other side. A prerequisite is that both parties should consider themselves as part of the team.

In difficult situations, a tendency to put the blame on the other person seems an easy route, which makes the situation even worse. It is in such moments that you may want to opt out of the relationship.

Opting out may seem the other easy route, but is certainly not so in reality. Instead of giving you the happiness that you desired so much, it may make you feel more hollow and unhappy. Be careful about making an impulsive decision.

Blaming your partner does not provide any solution if you plan to continue the relationship. Both parties need to first accept that they are in a situation that has been dealt to them by life, due to its forever changing property, and there is no point in playing the blame game. The next step is to address the situation with a focus on finding the right solution that serves everyone involved.

Choice 2 - After having followed your intentions for a long time, if you still feel that you and your partner have different outlooks and paths for your life's journey, then it is best to part without ill feelings.

You do have a choice at every step. So, please, for God's sake, do not ever put yourself in a victim syndrome, and do not say you do not know what to do about a relationship. You have a choice to keep it or terminate it.

Part-3

Relationships with Friends and Co-workers

Friends and co-workers form our peer groups, with whom we share similar interests and engage in similar activities.

We start forming friendships very early on in our developmental years with those who we find very similar to us, and whose company gives us a sense of happiness. Some of these friendships continue for life, some get lost on life's journey and new ones get formed. All through our life all those we consider our friends hold very special place in our heart.

Once we enter work force we start spending a big part of our daily life with our co-workers.

Health of these relationships is very important to our emotional health.

CHAPTER FIFTEEN

Relationship with Friends

The dictionary defines a friend as a person attached to another by feelings of affection or personal regard, a person who gives assistance; patron; supporter:

Friends are those who you hang out with; spend time with doing things, sharing thoughts and ideas.

You may have been trained to choose friends that care for you.

My suggestion - make friends with people who can gain in some way from your friendship, to whose life you can add some kind of value by providing company or advice, by doing certain tasks that would ease their life, by providing financial and emotional support when they need it, and, at times, by helping them make crucial choices when they face tough situations.

How does that generate a good feeling in you? Once you try this approach, you will know what I mean. Believe me, the most satisfying feeling in the world is when we can be of use to someone, add value in their life, and make them happy. It will raise your self-respect, make your life more meaningful, and provide a sense of purpose and achievement. And as long as you keep your intentions clear and pure and are not deterred by occasional disappointments, you will have long-lasting and genuine friendships. These friends will be the ones who will be there for you when you need them. They will be willing to go that extra mile to make you smile during rough times.

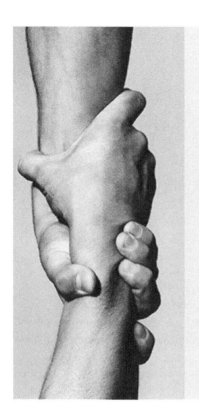

> **A real friend is who walks in when the rest of the world walks out**
>
> WALTER WINCHELL

CHAPTER SIXTEEN

Professional Relationships

You meet all kinds of personalities at work, as a boss, a co-worker, or a subordinate. Depending on the nature of your work, you may also interact with customers, vendors, suppliers, and contractors. Sometimes you are lucky to have good rapport, sometimes not.

The tips mentioned in Part 1 also help in an office environment.

First and foremost, be honest about your intention. You have a choice at the time of taking a job, because you like the kind of work you are expected to do and you like the culture of the company, and not because it offers a fat paycheck.

CHAPTER SEVENTEEN

Be Adaptable to change

To be successful at relationship management in an office setting, you need to be adaptable and tolerant. There are many factors that can change an office environment, such as a change of management, new office policies, and employee turnover.

In such situations we need to keep our focus on the ultimate goal that we are working towards – the goal of getting the job satisfaction. Establish good relationships with co-workers to create a congenial work environment, and be an effective contributor and good team player to get the best result.

If even after your best efforts to stay focused on your good intentions, the office environment becomes toxic, then you have a choice to continue or to leave the company and find a new job.

Sometimes it is not easy to leave. As mentioned earlier, if it is not possible to change a situation, then you have to accept it and create a mindset that you will not let your job impact your emotional health or your relationships negatively.

In Part 1, I wrote about my boss, Dan, who inspired me to

improve my disposition.

A few years later, I also had the experience of working with a manager who had a big ego and thought his main responsibility was to order people around. The successful completion of projects was not so much on his mind. He was more focused on how much fear he could create in his subordinates' minds.

He did not know how to motivate his team to perform better. His focus was on exercising his authority. He demanded respect and did not like it if anyone disagreed with him. The office environment became very toxic. There were times when I got into a defensive mode, and I did not like it.

This was also when I embarked on the journey of self-realization and consciously started diverting my thoughts from the feelings of being undervalued and disrespected to just enjoying my work. Interestingly, in a few months' time, that manager was transferred to another department, and our office environment improved significantly.

Putting pressure on subordinates never helps

When you put pressure on someone to perform as per your expectations or standards, you are not helping them perform better. Rather you are making them feel bad about themselves, and it lowers their self-confidence and their energy to be productive.

Putting pressure on subordinates to get work done is counterproductive. A whole new cycle of frustration and counter-productivity starts, which also affects otherwise beautiful relationships.

The best way to get anyone to perform as per your expectations is to first focus on their strengths. Compliment them. It will energize them. Then very lovingly, without being judgmental, without putting any blame or belittling, tell them what you expect of them. Only then, provide suggestions you may have for them to achieve their goals. They will welcome your suggestions once they are confident that you are not judging them and that you still love them unconditionally.

Open communication with a flow of unconditional love is the best way to have others respond to your expectations.

Everyone wants to perform to the best of their ability. Their focus or perception may be different from yours, or they may not have enough internal energy, which could be due to many factors, such as low self-confidence, guilt, fear, or hurt. At times, they may be hostile and rude with you. If they place you in high regard and you put pressure on them, they will feel more hurt now, and it will become a long-lasting scar in your beautiful relationship.

Also, please remember, when you expect someone else to do something beyond what they currently are doing to make you happy, it is an indicator that you are unhappy with your current situation. You have already let frustration creep into your state of mind, and that is not a happy state.

If you are the one who is being judged and someone is putting pressure on you, I suggest you understand that the other person is putting pressure on you because they themselves are feeling insecure. They do not have confidence in their abilities, and to prove their authority, they are trying these tactics.

The best approach in this case is to never try to defend yourself, even though you may feel that your ego and self-esteem is bruised. Don't focus on the fact that you are being misjudged or that someone is using their authority to pull you down. This will drain your energies and will make the situation worse. Instead, focus on feeling good and confident about your capabilities and try to finish the assigned task with full integrity. Also, do not change your attitude toward your manager by showing less respect or by being rude. Your behavior reflects your personality, and your bad behavior will add a feeling of guilt in your mind.

Ultimately, your manager will realize that they misjudged you, and they may even be impressed by your conduct and professional approach.

CHAPTER EIGHTEEN

Conclusion

We all need to nurture relationships by being open-minded, tolerant, and nonjudgmental. We need to understand that each one of us is different and unique, and each one of us has something to contribute—that is what makes life beautiful. We should respect this diversity and enjoy it.

My mantra: Every interaction offers an opportunity to learn something. Identify what you can learn.

Our relationships are generated from our thoughts. Our relationships are a mirror of how we think about ourselves and about others. When you acknowledge and accept that you, and only you, have control of your feelings, you will be able to find solutions to all the problems in your relationships. You will be able to pick, develop, and maintain your relationships as you choose.

"There isn't time, so brief is life, for bickering, apologies, heartburnings, callings to account. There is only time for loving, and but an instant, so to speak, for that." – Mark Twain

Acknowledgements

First and foremost, to Nicole C. Ayers, for providing her timely support in editing and polishing this book with her incredible attention to detail and full command of the English language.

And I want to thank and acknowledge wonderful Molly Ahuja for reviewing it for the last-minute edits and providing consultation and invaluable feedback.

About the Author
Nimi Kay was inspired to write this book based on her journey of learning the nuances of healthy relationships. Growing up, Nimi felt melancholy and discouraged most of the time. She attributed this to being misunderstood by others or not being loved enough by others. In her quest to find a way to get rid of these feelings, she discovered that her thoughts and the frequency of her body's energy were the cause of suffering and not any external forces. She also realized that one could learn to manage these feelings if one became aware of one's thoughts and feelings as they happen.

With practice, Nimi learned that one could live a blissful and happy life despite challenges in relationships. Now she enjoys her beautiful relationship with herself and the world around her and lives a blissful life.

Made in the USA
Monee, IL
04 March 2023

29144011R10080